# A SHORT SKETCH OF THE LIFE AND WORK OF GURU GOBIND SINGH

# A SHORT SKETCH OF THE LIFE AND WORK OF GURU GOBIND SINGH

## THE 10TH AND LAST GURU OF THE SIKHS,

BY


BHAGAT LAKSHMAN SINGH,

DISTRICT INSPECTOR OF SCHOOLS, LUDHIANA,
LATE PROFESSOR OF HISTORY AND ENGLISH LITERATURE, GORDON MISSION COLLEGE, RAWALPINDI,
FORMERLY MEMBER, KHALSA COLLEGE COUNCIL,
LATE EDITOR OF "THE KHALSA."



GYAN

*Published by*

GYAN

Gyan Publishing House
5, Ansari Road
Daryaganj, New Delhi-110002
Phone: 011-47034999, 9811692060
E-mail: books@gyanbooks.com

*Distribution Network*
gyanbooks.com
India, USA, Canada, UK, Australia, France



ISBN : 978-81-212-4009-3 (PB)
First Published, 1909

2nd Impression 2020

*Printed at:* Gyan Press, Delhi.



**A**
**Short Sketch of The Life and Work of Guru Gobind Singh**
Author: Bhagat Lakshman Singh

# A

SHORT SKETCH

OF

# THE LIFE AND WORK

OF

# Guru Gobind Singh

THE 10TH AND LAST GURU OF THE SIKHS,

BY

BHAGAT LAKSHMAN SINGH,

DISTRICT INSPECTOR OF SCHOOLS, LUDHIANA,

LATE PROFESSOR OF HISTORY AND ENGLISH LITERATURE, GORDON MISSION COLLEGE, RAWALPINDI,
FORMERLY MEMBER, KHALSA COLLEGE COUNCIL,
LATE EDITOR OF "THE KHALSA."

1909.

*Páin gaé jab té tumré,*
*Tab té koú ánkh taré nahín ányon.*

"Lord, since I took shelter at thy feet,
I have not noticed anyone!"

*Ehai káj dhará ham janamam,*
*Samajh leo Sádhú sab manamam,*
*Dharm chaláwan sant ubháran,*
*Dusht sabhan ko múl upáran.*

"For this purpose was I born,
Understand all ye pious people!
To inaugurate righteousness, to lift up the good,
To destroy all evil-doers, root and branch!"

*Kahiyo Prabhú so bhákh hún.*
*Kisú na kán rákh hún.*

"As the Lord told me I say.
I do not fear any one."

Guru Govind Singh.

## BHAGAT BALMUKAND, B.A., LL.B.,

(*Died October 3rd*, 1904).

PLEADER, CHIEF COURT, PUNJAB.

Beloved Brother,

For thy amiability and specklessly pure life, thy selfless patriotism, and thy devout regard for India's great men, I take the liberty to dedicate to thy sacred memory my this humble effort to sketch the life and work of one of the greatest of India's sons. In life, though thou wast yet hardly 30, thy "kathás" from the Upnishads, and the Maha-Bharata raised the spirits and gladdened the hearts of the congregations of thy townsmen and towns-women. I trust that, in death, through this humble work, thou mayst bear a message of hope and cheer to the down-trodden and the lowly of this unfortunate action-ridden land of social and religious tyranny and of superstition and oppression.

March 10th, 1909, A. D. LAKSHMAN SINGH.

# INTRODUCTION.

Bhagat Lakshman Singh, the writer of the memoir, has chosen to remember me kindly in connection with his conception of this work and now insists on my writing a preface in spite of my lack of leisure and occupation of mind with matters other than literary. Though yielding to his persistence I regret very much that I shall not be able to convey to the readers what I have felt, for many years now, about the subject of this sketch. Guru Govind Singh has been a unique personality in history, the full bearing of whose life has yet to be realized. Born in a family of rulers of men's mind, at a time of great difficulty in the history of his country, amongst a community of oppressed, depressed and disorganised people, he showed himself equal to the occasion and has left indelible marks on the march of events. What a difficult position had he and how did he acquit himself?—sums up the life of this one of the greatest of the human-born. He was born to a *gaddi* of a succession of saints, whose high and unblemished lives, whose unique and unrivalled teachings, whose position as protectors and saviors he had to continue under much more complex conditions and in awkward times. He was not to succeed to a *gaddi* of *ascetics*, but to marry, rear up children and see their end. He was to succeed to a position of wealth, power and affluence, all of which he had to administer not for his own and his family's good but for the good of the community. He had to receive homage from the rulers and the ruled, the rich and the poor, the good and the bad, the high and the low, and to keep his head calm and cool. He had the choice of perpetuating the succession of his family, he had the option of incorporating himself with the mightiest of the land and the times, he had the temptation to wreck the work of generations; what he did actually in these matters is well known and needs no repetition, Shew me a man in the history of the world in such a difficult position and with such a splendid record. Of this man Bhagat Lakshman Singh writes and writes as a believer. Many others will follow and write philosophically, critically and with more materials at their disposal and show that Guru Govind Singh was a saint, scholar, soldier, statesman and Saviour, the like of which may not come again.

LAHORE: 14*th March*, 1909. HARKISHEN LAL,

# PREFACE.

Of all works on Sikh history compiled by European authors not one contains a comprehensive account of the life of Guru Govind Singh, the 10th and last Guru of the Sikhs. As a rule these writers have commenced their works from the time of Baba Nanak, the founder of the Sikh creed, and have ended them with a brief reference to the political convulsions of the period in which the 10th Guru played not a small part. They believed, along with the majority of the Indian writers, that the principal work of the Guru was of a political nature and by giving him credit for this they thought that they had said all that could be said of him. This, I submit, is too poor a tribute to the memory of the Guru. I have tried to show, in this memoir, that his military achievements were only a chapter in his life and that his great and lasting work was to preach the Fatherhood of God and the Brotherhood of man, whereby he infused true manliness into the hearts of the people of this land. I have endeavoured to write a simple, readable and believable story of the Guru's life and have based it mainly on the Dassam Granth which contains writings believed to have been written by the Guru himself. I have referred to the contemporary and later Moslem historians and English writers on Indian history and, where necessary, I have quoted largely from them to corroborate what I have said. I have visited several of the Gurudwaras and places of note with which the memory of the Guru is associated, and have personally enquired into the traditions that are current there. In a word, I have done all that my humble resources could permit me to do. I do not, of course, believe that I have said all that could be said about the Guru, or that I have exhausted all sources of information in writing this work. I have only attempted to place in the hands of the English knowing public a handy book containing a simple narrative of the life of one who is regarded as Saviour by millions of men, inhabiting the land of the Five Waters. I feel confident that my humble effort will stimulate an interest in the work of the Divine Poet, Sage, Reformer, Patriot and Martyr, and that abler and better informed men will feel encouraged to write a comprehensive account of his life.

The Persian passage on pages 51 and 52 and its translation have been taken from a paper contributed to the "Tribune", some 3 years back. The Persian extract on page 44 has been inserted on the authority of a Muslim friend. I have not been able to verify the authorship of these passages. Some friends have just told me that Sundri Devi, and not Jitoji, was the Guru's first wife. The suggestion has come too late for the institution of an enquiry. The battle of Bhangáni has been purposely described along with other battles of the Guru with the hill Rajas, for the sake of the tenor of the story. Though it had taken place sometime before the foundation of the "Panth," its cause was the same—the resentment of the hill Rajas at the Guru's efforts to infuse military spirit into his followers and to march, at times, in military array.

LAHORE: \
*March* 10*th*, 1909. } LAKSHMAN SINGH.

# INTRODUCTION.

"God creates saints from age to age", say our Scriptures, "and preserves virtue."* The history of the human race bears abundant testimony to the truth embodied in these words. How Gautam Budha preached love and sympathy, how Christ was crucified while striving to teach the lessons of charity and righteous dealing, how, again, the Sufis have endeavoured to mollify the stubborn hearts of many a follower of the Crescent, are matters of history. Guru Govind Singh's mission was exactly the same. He brought the same message and received martyrdom when communicating it. The same scene is enacted in the drama of human life from age to age. The part played is the same, more or less. Only the time, stage, and actors are different.

The story of Guru Govind Singh's life is at once pathetic and heart-stirring. Bereft of his saintly father, when yet a child, troubled by jealous kinsmen, persecuted by unscrupulous foes, and betrayed by false friends, he lived to be able to procure freedom for his countrymen from the tyrannous political yoke of the Mughal and the demoralizing spiritual subjection of the Brahman. He swerved not from duty He communicated his message boldly and fearlessly.

The times of his advent were very hard. The Hindu social system had deadened the hearts of people. Each individual lived for himself. The feelings of

* Jug Jug Bhagat Upáindá paij rakhdà áiyá.

manliness and sympathy were gone. A desire to avenge wrong was not felt. Even a wild mouse presents a bold front to the enemy when he stands at bay. But, thanks to the framers and administrators of the Hindu law, the whole mass of the humanity, within the Hindu pale, had become inanimate, as it were. Its men were taken into captivity and women sold in the frontier markets; but it moved not. In addition to the calamities that the Punjab Hindus suffered from being exposed to the frequent inroads of the Muslim invaders they had to put up with constant insults at the hands of the Muslim officials and nobles. Life and property were not safe. Young, unmarried, beautiful Hindu girls were forcibly taken away from their parents and guardians. Marrige parties were waylaid. Bride-grooms were assassinated and their brides were snatched from them. The Hindu places of worship were desecrated; but no notice was taken of the conduct of the ruffians who did so. A regular campaign, under official patronage, was going on to forcibly convert the Hindus to the Muslim Faith; and, thus, brothers were torn from brothers, fathers and mothers from their sons and daughters. Those who refused were tortured to death. All Hindu hearths were houses of mourning. A constant wail went forth from the Hindu Punjab. The unfortunate, oppressed people found consolation in their religion. They attributed their troubles to Fate and resigned themselves to Fate. They thought they were being punished for their 'Karmas', in previous births, and that their oppressors were not to blame! They were only instruments in the hands of God! What other attitude could be adopted by a people who had become mentally so low as to acquiesce in the belief that even Pars Ram, who is said to have annihilated the whole Kshatrya race, was an incarnation of Vishnu and was, as such, entitled to their homage!

On this heart-rending scene Guru Govind Singh appeared, as a healer, to preach a new Gospel to the oppressed humanity. He told them to discard their worthless old beliefs† and to throw themselves on the mercy of the Gracious Providence and they would be saved. "Sin and suffering approach not those who meditate on the Lord's name" was the message he brought. He made them understand that all suffering was the result of their own failings, that God sent no trouble, that the oppressors were not His instruments, that they should believe in one God and should love one another as brothers, that they should rise together and fall together, that they should resist and root out all evil-doers, that they should not fear death, and that they should regard life only as a means to an end—to attain beatitude at the feet of the Timeless One. He died in order that God's people should live. Those who heard the message were saved. Hindu brothers, you have disowned your Saviour!

LAHORE;
*Dated March 10th*, 1909. } LAKSHMAN SINGH,

---

†Phokat dharm na kandí káman.

## THE AUTHOR'S OBLIGATIONS.

I am indebted to my esteemed friend, Hon'ble Lala Harkishen Lal, B. A., Barrister-at-Law, Cantab, the great pioneer of industrial progress in the Punjab, for the conception and publication of this work. It was he who, eight years back, put the idea into my head to record what I knew of the Guru and it is, again, he who has borne the expenses of its publication and has arranged for its sale on cost price. The major portion of the book was written, six years back, when my time was my own and it would have been published the same year; but it was my desire to first show it to some friends with a view to get language and style improved, so far as possible. My friends, Indians and Europeans both, have not, for some reason or other, been helpful in this matter. So the book appears before the public mainly as it was written. The only Sikh who has been of some assistance to me in going through the proofs and giving several useful suggestions is my young friend and pupil, Bhai Jodh Singh, M. A, Professor of Divinity, Khalsa College, Amritsar, to whom my acknowledgments are due. Under the circumstances it must be full of imperfections; but if the admirers and disciples of the Guru kindly favour me with their suggestions the 2nd edition may be comparatively a flawless one.

LAHORE;
*March* 10*th*, 1909 *A. D.*

LAKSHMAN SINGH.

# CONTENTS.

CHAPTER XI.

## CHAPTER XVIII.



## CHAPTER XIX.



## CHAPTER XX.



## CHAPTER XXI.



## CHAPTER XXII.

## CHAPTER XXIII.



## CHAPTER XXIV.



## CHAPTER XXV.



## CHAPTER XXVI.



## CHAPTER XXVII.



## CHAPTER XXVIII.



## CHAPTER XXIX.



## CHAPTER XXX.

# CHAPTER—I.

GURU GOBIND SINGH was born on Friday the 13th of Poh, Sudi 7th, Samvat Vikrimaditya 1723, according to 1666 A.D. at Patna, a large town of historic renown, in the Province of Behar. His father, Guru Tegh Bahadur, was absent at the time, at Kamrup, in Assam, where he had gone with Raja Bishen Singh of Jodhpur whom he had helped in the conquest of that Province and who subsequently became his very ardent follower. Both at Patna and Kamrup great rejoicings took place to mark this auspicious event. From all parts of the country the Guru's followers flocked to Patna to see their future Guru and to make their offerings in cash and kind. Gobind Singh's maternal uncle, Kirpal Chand, received them kindly and sent them back loaded with favours. After the lapse of eleven months Guru Tegh Bahadur halted at Patna to see his family and the newly-born babe with whom the Providence had blessed him and who was destined to add lustre to his already illustrious name. After a brief sojourn he proposed to his mother and to his wife that they should return to Anandpur which he had himself built, for his residence, on the spurs of the Himalayas; but the ladies preferred the quiet of Patna where no ill-feeling could be excited in the breasts of their jealous kinsmen and where the plots and intrigues of Ram Rai and other Sodhi claimants to the *Gaddi* could do them no

---

* *According to some writers the Guru went to Bhutan and not to Assam.*

harm. So the Guru returned alone to Anandpur to the great dismay of the men who had consoled themselves with the belief that he had left the Punjab for good and who were making strenuous efforts to prevail upon Aurangzebe to confer the vacant *Gaddi* on Ram Rai, and to the boundless joy of his adherents who came in large numbers to welcome him back in their midst and to receive from him the solace of religion. The devoted worshippers brought with them the offerings they had deposited for years and built spacious mansions for the visitors and the Guru's family.

Anandpur, in those days, was exactly the place of bliss, as its name implies. Guru Tegh Bahadur was a saint immensely rich in the love of God and man. His days and nights were mostly spent either in meditation or in preaching to all who came to him that this world and its ties were transient, that only the Lord's name was real and that real happiness lay not in the enjoyment of gross earthly pleasures but in losing one's self in the contemplation of the Creator. His writings are throughout imbued with transcendental spirituality. No sooner the eye rests on them, or the ear hears them recited, a thrill runs through one's whole frame. The grosser nature seems then to be entirely subdued in the holy presence; and though when this sacred influence is removed it may recover its power over the frail man, it may be said with justice that for the time the sacred influence lasts the worshipper feels, as it were, completely purified and fit to be received into the bosom of the Father. When this is the influence of the Guru's writings the force of his presence can well be imagined. No wonder, then, that the whole of Northern India hankering after spiritual knowledge should have sought relief in pilgrimage to Anandpur; and if it can be supposed that God incarnates or sends his chosen into this world to better the condition of the fallen humanity Guru Tegh Bahadur certainly deserved to be favoured with a son worthy of being entrusted with a divine mission.

When the Guru was engaged in ministering to the spiritual wants of his followers at Anandpur his son, Govind Singh, was being brought up at Patna, under the care of his mother, grandmother and uncle Kirpal Chand. He remained here about five years. The writers of Sikh chronicles say that, when a child at Patna, Govind Singh developed features which showed unmistakably that he was destined to be a leader of men. He gathered round himself boys of his age and played various games with them. He organised boat races, arranged mimic fights and handsomely rewarded those who won. In a word he had made himself so famous, even as a child, and had endeared himself so much to all who came in contact with him that, when pressed by the importunities of his followers, Guru Tegh Bahadur sent for him to Anandpur, the men and women of Patna, young and old, became disconsolate. Little did they think, perhaps, that the child, who in parting from them pained them so deeply, would grow to be so famous and that Patna, as his birth place, would be associated with his name as long as Sikh history lasted and would become a seat of pilgrimage for ages to come. At Anandpur Govind Singh's arrival was hailed with joy. Immense multitudes thronged on the roads and in the temple to have the privilege of casting first glance on him. Guru Tegh Bahadur solemnised this occasion by offering thanksgivings to the Father Almighty and feeding thousands of the poor. The news of Govind Singh's arrival soon spread far and near and disciples from Multan and Sindh, Kabul and Kandhar, Dhani and Pothohar and other parts of the Punjab brought for him all sorts of presents. These he distributed amongst his playmates. The gifts included horses of the choicest breed from Khorasan and Persia and arrows and weapons of the rarest make from Kabul and Kandhar. The future founder of the Sikh military power prized these gifts most and even at that age he took special delight in organising an army of irregulars and in roaming about the jungles at their head in search of *Shikar*. His handsome face, his princely bearing, his kind look, his sweet Patna dialect, made still sweeter when it proceeded from his sweet lips, his pleasing manners and his winning smile made him a universal favourite. The calls on his time were so many that his mother and grandmother often complained that he stayed out for the greater part of the day. At the age of seven he was placed under the tutelage of Sahib Chand Granthi to learn Gurmukhi in company with Manya who, under the name of Mani Singh, subsequently played an important part in Sikh history and died as a martyr, Nand Chand, his future councillor and his other playmates. Gifted as he was with an extraordinary genius he completely learnt the Ad Granth in a short time, and his recitations elicited popular applause. In the same year Qazi Pir Mohammed was appointed to teach him Persian and an expert Rajput was entrusted with the duty of training him in horsemanship and in the use of weapons.

From the worldly point of view this may be regarded as the happiest period of Govind Singh's life. All that man could desire was his. His father was the spiritual ruler of men or *Sacha Padshah*, the real King, by which name he was remembered by the Sikh disciples. His mother and grand-mother were adored by millions of men and women. His mornings and evenings were spent in devotion and days in *Shikar* and other manly games. At night before he went to bed, in the palatial residence set apart for him, numerous attendants sang for him hymns from Granth Sahib and made a paradise, as it were, of his home. But it was not for these earthly blessings and worldly enjoyments that God had sent him into this world. So before he completed his ninth year all this vista of human bliss vanished and the stern Providence called him to duty.

# CHAPTER—II.

ALAMGIR AURANGZEBE, the Moghal Emperor, came to the throne by imprisoning his aged father; and to secure it to himself he had the saintly Dara Shikoh, his elder brother, and the timid Murad, his younger brother, cruelly murdered. The third brother, Shujah, fled to Arakan where he died miserably. These crimes, though, not so uncommon in those days, created indignation throughout the Muslim world. For the murder of Dara Shikoh he put forward the excuse that he had become a Sufi and had died the death of a heretic. But for other misdeeds he could render no satisfactory explanation. Discontent, therefore, brewed near his throne and in the remote provinces. The Moghal officers in Deccan, Bengal, Oudh, Punjab and Kabul lost faith in the occupant of the Delhi throne and began to devise ways and means for shaking off their allegiance. "The Sheriff of Mecca refused to receive his envoys although they brought him money presents. Shah Abbas of Persia hated Aurangzebe and severely condemned him for his treatment of his father and his brethren. He scoffed at the title which Aurangzebe had assumed of "Conqueror of the World"; and he threatened to march an army to Delhi. Aurangzebe was in the utmost alarm"*—

In this plight Aurangzebe took shelter with *Ulemas* and professors of his religion and by their sympathy, which he purchased by the free

* *J. T. Wheeler, A short History of India, pages 163 and 170.*

bestowal of royal favours, he began to play the rôle of the Defender of Islam. To pander to the prejudices of the fanatical mob, quite against the conciliatory policy of his three illustrious predecessors, he began to rule his vast empire, inhabited by a population of diverse creeds and races, by organising a regular *Jehad* against all non-Muslims. Orders were issued that thenceforward no non-Muslim should be appointed to any Civil or Military office; that Lambardars and Zaildars should all be Muslims; that Sanskrit should not be taught; that Hindus should not be allowed to go on pilgrimage to their time-honoured shrines. All sorts of oppressive taxes were levied on non-Muslims and, when these sources of tyranny were exhausted, he ordered the forcible conversion of the Hindus. The worship of idols was made a crime. The temples of the non-Muslims were demolished and mosques were substituted in their place, some of which may still be seen in different parts of India. "Instead of permitting the followers of other religions to worship God in their own way, Aurangzebe sought to force them into becoming Muhammadans. He began by destroying idols and pagodas within his own territories and building up mosques in their room. He burnt down a great pagoda near Delhi. He converted a magnificent temple at Mathra into a mosque. He drove religious mendicants of every idolatrous sect out of Hindustan. He ordered the Viceroys of provinces to carry on the same work throughout the Empire. At the same time he prohibited the celebration of the Hindu festivals. He required all Hindu servants of the Moghal Government to become Muhammadans under pain of losing their appointments. He imposed the *Jezya* on all his subjects who refused to become Muhammadans. Even the English and Dutch residents in India were subjected to the same obnoxious impost. The Rana of Udaipur was ordered to allow cows to be slaughtered in his territories"*.—

When this was the attitude of the head of the Empire the atrocities committed, in the name of religion, by petty potentates in the provinces, may well be imagined. *Kalima* or the sword was the option given to non-Muslims. A story, somewhat exaggerated, is told that in those days, Aurangzebe had resolved that he would not take his breakfast unless one and a quarter maund sacred threads were brought to him daily and their wearers made Muslims. In Kashmere the Governor Sher Afgan forcibly converted half the population to Islam. The chosen few among the rest took shelter with Guru Tegh Bahadur. It is stated by some that the Kashmiri Pundits were advised to seek the Guru's aid by the deity presiding over the shrine of Amar Nath, in the north-west of Kashmir: and by others that the Guru's kinsmen, burning with the fire of envy and labouring under the mortification they had experienced in the complete failure of their efforts to obtain the *Gaddi*, put this idea into the head of the defenceless Kashmiris to involve Guru

---

* *Talboy's Wheeler, a short History of India pages 177-78.*

Tegh Bahadur into a quarrel with the great Moghal whose might would ultimately crush him and make it impossible for his descendants to retain hold over the *Gaddi*. Be that as it may, the Guru received them most kindly. Their tale of woe melted him into tears. For a long time he remained speechless. When at last he composed himself he gravely replied that, until some virtuous person sacrificed himself at the altar of Faith, God's people would find no rest. Silence prevailed in the audience. Govind Singh was then nine years old. Respectfully leaving the lap of his father and kneeling before him he said "Sire, thou art an embodiment of virtue. Give thy life for these poor people. Who else will protect them?" These brave words from a child of nine years addressed to the parent into whose lap he had been playing a few minutes previous, spread a feeling of wonder and amazement into the whole audience. They stared now into the face of the father and then into that of the son and began to feel a sort of supernatural awe in their presence. There was, however, little cause for wonderment in what they witnessed. Both these, father and son, had been sent into this world for a special purpose, the fulfilment of which necessitated extraordinary courage and sacrifice. With these manly virtues they were most thoroughly endowed. Both were conscious of the mighty revolutions that the Divine Ruler had ordained through them and both were completely resigned to His will.

The speech of Govind Singh received a ready response. Guru Tegh Bahadar asked the Kashmiri Pundits to write to the Emperor that in case His Majesty prevailed upon their leader, Guru Tegh Bahadur, to become a Mussalman they would all accept the *Kalima* of the Prophet; otherwise they should be allowed to worship their gods as before. The Kashmiri Pundits, reduced to desperation though they were, for a while hesitated in submitting such a petition. They had, of course, come to seek the Guru's aid; but nothing was further from their intention than to involve a saint like the Guru into such a serious difficulty. Superstitious to the extreme they had thought that by some miraculous agency the Guru would avert the calamity that faced them. But to their horror the blessed saint recommended a course which simply meant death to him. At length, pressed by the Sodhi enemies of the Guru, to whom his death was most welcome, they yielded. The petition was accordingly sent to the Imperial Potentate through Zalim Khan, Subah of the Punjab. On receipt of it Aurangzebe called a meeting of the *Ulemas* and Qazis of his court and asked their opinion. All were agreed that it would be a matter for congratulation if by one man's conversion millions of infidels entered the fold of Islam. As a result of this deliberation two special messengers were sent to bring Guru Tegh Bahadar to Delhi. The Guru, however, preferred not to go with the Imperial guards. He sent back the emissaries of Aurangzebe with the reply that he would come attended by his own men.

Very soon after he made preparations for his departure and gave instructions to Govind Singh as to how the work was to be carried on during his absence. His parting with his mother and his wife was simply pathetic. The mother's heart gave way at the thought that her son was leaving her to come no more. The wife was quiet; but her reserve distinctly betrayed how she felt her lord's separation. The Guru consoled them by reciting several hymns of his own composition which all inculcated that this world was a sort of a *Serai* where men stopped, for a while, on their way home. Their ties were transient. Father, son, mother, child, husband, wife, all were bound together by selfish instincts. In time of prosperity they were all friends, but in adversity all fled away. That the only object of love should be God Almighty who was real and eternal friend. In this way taking leave of his family and followers the Guru started for Delhi. On his way he halted at various places and preached God's name to the people. This caused delay. Aurangzebe was persuaded to believe that the Guru was hiding himself for fear. Messengers were sent in all directions to search for him. A prize was set on his head. Meanwhile the Guru was proceeding in the direction of Delhi by slow marches. But before he reached there he changed his mind and went to Agra instead. Why he adopted the latter course is difficult to account for. The Sikh writers say that an old lady of Agra, Bhago by name, a disciple of Guru Arjan, longed to see him. Also that one

Hassan Ali, an impecunious Syad, old and decrepit, hearing that a handsome reward was set on the Guru's head prayed that if, as people said, the Guru was a friend of the poor and knower of hearts, instead of surrendering himself to the Moghal Emperor he would come to him so that, by handing him over to the Imperial authorities, he might get the promised reward and thereby relieve the burden of his old age. To satisfy the craving of these two persons the Guru went to Agra where he was arrested in a garden, in the suburbs of Agra, and was imprisoned in the local fortress.

When the incident was reported to Aurangzebe he was overjoyed at the thought that now, through the Guru of the Hindus, he would succeed in converting countless men to the creed of Islam. The Guru was taken to Delhi under Imperial escort. Through the advice of the Head Qazi he was lodged in a dilapidated building, supposed to be haunted by evil spirits where, according to the popular belief, many persons had been tormented to death. But no evil genius molested the Guru. Next morning the Guru was presented to Aurangzebe who received him with honour and implored him to lend the weight of his influence in his policy of conversion. The Indian peoples, he said, were hopelessly divided into numberless creeds which resulted in mutual hatred and internecine quarrels and caused countless difficulties to the Government. If people believed in one religion they would live in peace and accord. The Guru, as a successor of Baba Nanak, should hail the prospect of his people giving up idols and believing in one God. Should the Guru proffer him the required assistance he would give him a lady of the royal household in marriage, make him Nawab of the Punjab or, if he so elected, he would issue a decree that the whole of Muslim India should regard him as their premier *Pir*. He felt confident that even if the Guru did not feel inclined to accept the *Kalima* he would acknowledge the Prophet for the sake of the millions of the Hindus who were suffering no end of persecution on account of their refusal to avail themselves of the blessings of Islam. Men of his stamp laid down their lives for the sake of others. In the present instance no demand was made on his life. A little inconvenience to him would result in a blessing to millions of his fellow-men who would obtain peace in this life and paradise in the next. Should he, however, choose to refuse the offer he would meet death at the hands of the public executioner.

The Guru heard the speech of the astute Moghal with perfect serenity. He calmly replied that it was a mistaken policy to compel people to change their faith. A belief in this or that creed did not entitle any one to a seat in Heaven. To God Mussalmans and Hindus were all alike. It was blind fanaticism that led men to believe that God was partial to one creed and inimical to another. Entry into Heaven rested on one's actions and not on lip professions. To him the pleasures of this life had little charm. He had no ambition to contract matrimonial ties with the royal family or to wield spiritual sway by the aid of an Imperial decree. He was completely resigned to the will of God, and in Divine grace alone lay the fruition of his desires. He was not afraid of death. Death was only the inevitable dissolution of the elements of which the body was composed. Rama had passed away. Rawan with his large offspring had met a similar fate. The world was like a dream and nothing in it was stable. Anxiety need be felt for what was an unusual catastrophe. Whoever was born must die sometime or other. He had given up all worldly entanglements and had taken to the singing of the Lord's glory.

Finding that the Guru could not be won over by smooth speech Aurangzebe ordered his subjection to torture in the vilest of dungeons so that physical suffering might compel him to embrace Islam. Diwan Mati Ram, Bhai Gurditta, Bhai Dyala, uncle of Mania, Bhai Udai and Bhai Jaita, Mazhabi Sikhs, who had accompanied the Guru from Anandpur were incarcerated in separate rooms. The dungeon-keepers impressed by the Guru's holy presence gave him no trouble. They quietly sat outside and the messengers from Anandpur, sent by mother Nanaki, and the Sikh disciples from Delhi were freely admitted to pay their homage to the Guru. A few days after, the Guru, together with his companions, was taken to the royal presence. Aurangzebe again called upon the party to give up their false creed. Diwan Mati Ram said, by way of retort, that it was Islam that was false and not the Sikh creed. If God had viewed Islam with favour he would have created all men circumcised.

The Diwan's boldness cost him his life. An infernal machine was immediately erected in the Diwan Khana and Mati Ram was forthwith sawn into pieces. Aurangzebe and his hardened courtiers stood emotionless. Their diabolic looks, on the contrary, betrayed inward satisfaction. Bhai Dyala, unable to control himself, gave vent to his feelings by calling Aurangzebe a tyrant. He cursed him for committing such atrocities in the name of God and religion and predicted the rapid fall of his dynasty. Aurangzebe was all wrath. The court parasites still more furious. The Bhai was dragged out of court and thrown into a boiling cauldron. The royal monster then turned upon the Guru and dismissed him by saying that if he did not accept Islam he too would meet similar fate. Next day Bhai Gurditta approached the Guru and proposed a means of escape from the prison. The Guru, perceiving his motive, permitted him and his other two companions to return to their homes. Somehow they escaped from the prison, but with remorse they returned and stayed with the Guru till his death.

When the news of the martyrdom of Diwan Mati Ram and Bhai Dyala reached Anandpur mother Nanaki was filled with alarm regarding the safety of her son. Overpowered by continued anxiety and sorrow she sought relief in frequent attempts to proceed to Delhi. Govind Singh, however, informed timely, invariably prevailed upon her to desist from the resolve and to have the satisfaction that her son was courting a death that was nobler than life itself. The Guru, too, thought so. Aurangzebe's threat failed in its effect and the prospect of the Guru's conversion was as remote as ever. Sedate and calm he waited for his end patiently. One day when he was attending to his toilette on the roof of his dungeon, he cast a look towards the south. The matter was brought to the notice of Aurangzebe who sent for him and accused him of looking at the ladies of the Imperial palace. The Guru is said to have calmly replied that he had been looking in the direction of the sea from where a white race would come, take possession of the Moghal throne and violate the sanctity of the royal seraglio.

The prophecy excited a furious uproar. Both the King and the courtiers showered imprecations on the hoary-headed saint. The cries of "down with the infidel!" "Kill the prating Kafir!" filled the air. The Guru was accordingly condemned to die and was beheaded publicly in Chandni Chauk on the 13th of Maghar 1732 Vik., Sudi 5, according to 1675 A. D. The kind hearted among the by-standers, Muslims or non-Muslims, could not restrain shedding a tear of sympathy. The whole country was convulsed, from one end to the other. In the words of Govind Singh "A wail went forth from the denizens of the globe and hail!, hail!, hail!, was heard from on high." And though the statement of the Sikh writers that when the Guru died a strong wind blew, earthquakes shook the globe, many houses fell and the whole nature seemed to have been disturbed may savour of exaggeration there is no doubt that the beheading of Guru Tegh Bahadur alienated the sympathies of millions of men and the Empire of the Moghals received a rude shock.

* NOTE.—A Durbar was held at Delhi, in honour of the coronation of His Majesty, King-Emperor Edward, during the first ten days of January, 1903. The author of this memoir happened to be there on the occasion. On the 6th idem, the morning of Guru Govind Singh's Birth Anniversary, that was celebrated in the Shahid Ganj, seat of martyrdom of Guru Tegh Bahadur, the Sikh princes came in state to pay their homage to the shrine. Among the sight-seers were the special correspondents of about twelve Anglo-Indian and English journals. The following extract from the report of the celebrations published in the *Times of India*, Bombay, dated January 14th, 1903, will shew the extent of the grateful feeling the visit to the Shahid Ganj evoked in the breasts of the English correspondents :—

"Two hundred and twenty-seven years ago a Guru, or an apostle of the Sikhs, was in captivity in a small building in Chandni Chauk, at Delhi. He was Guru Tegh Bahadur, the ninth in succession of the great Gurus who welded the Sikhs into a band of Asiatic Iron-sides, inspired by pure religious zeal, made valiant by the most rigorous military discipline. Tegh Bahadur had fallen into the clutches of the great Emperor Aurangzebe who was eager to compass his doom. At last a false charge was trumped up against him. He was accused of having, when outside his prison, stared curiously in the direction of the great Moghal's Zenana. Questioned as to his alleged crime he answered loudly 'I was not looking towards the zenana. I was looking south for the white race who are coming from beyond the sea to tear down thy pardahs and to destroy thine empire.' The words sealed his doom. He was taken back to the dungeon and beheaded by the order of the incensed potentate. But his words lived in the memory of the persecuted Sikhs. His prophecy was spread, far and wide, by Govind Singh, the 10th and greatest Guru, who finally consolidated the Sikhs into a religious and political power, destined to become dominant, when the Moghal Empire crumbled to pieces. And on the day when John Nicholson led the assault on Delhi, which ended the Moghal reign for ever, the Sikh troops who helped to storm the breaches shouted aloud the prophecy of their martyred Guru. To-day was the Birth day of Govind Singh, an anniversary held sacred by all Sikhs, when they meet in their temples to offer prayers to his memory. It was decided by the leading Sikh Maharajas now at the Imperial assemblage to go in solemn procession to the shrine of Tegh Bahadur and to do homage to the name of Govind Singh and renew their vows of loyalty to the King-Emperor upon that venerated spot. For the little prison is now a temple and place of pilgrimage, hallowed by the people, for whose sake the saintly Guru died. The ceremony was witnessed by about a dozen Europeans for it had not been publicly announced. But thousands of Sikhs from all over Northern India were there, drawn together by a common motive. It was one of the most dramatic events of this eventful gathering. For this Darbar marks the final fulfilment of the prophecy. Here in Imperial Delhi the monarch of the 'White Race from over the Sea' has just proclaimed his right to rule over a vaster empire than the Moghals ever knew. By the aid of the gallant Sikhs the prediction has been fulfilled to the letter. And it was a sight worth seeing, that of the Sikhs flocking to do homage to the King-Emperor upon the very spot where their leader laid down his life for his faith. It was something that a patriotic Englishman remembering how completely the vision of the Guru had been realised, could not contemplate without a thrill of pride. . . . . When you thought of the martyred ascetic, of his vision of the White Race from over the ocean, of the gallant Sikhs fighting for Great Britain in the streets of Delhi, and last and strongest sight of all, of the Sikhs themselves saluting their sacred book that morning with the British National Anthem, you felt that here was a moving picture which, could they but see it, might well give pause to the enemies of England."

# CHAPTER—III.

In the midst of the confusion which was caused, when Guru Tegh Bahadur was beheaded, his head, which had fallen at some distance from the place of execution, was at once picked up by Bhai Jaita and taken to Anandpur where it was cremated with due honours. His body lay in the dungeon. When in the dusk of the evening Lakhi, a follower of the Guru and arsenal contractor, was returning from the fort, with seven hundred empty carts, Bhai Udai proposed to him to remove the Guru's remains. The proposal was agreed to. What for the dusk of the evening and what for the clouds of dust stirred up by so many vehicles the body was removed unobserved into a cart and taken with the greatest possible speed to Rakab Ganj about 4 miles from the place of execution. The other carts followed at their usual speed. When they were gone and the dust cleared and the sentinels noticed the feat the matter was reported to the authorities. A detachment of cavalry was sent in pursuit; but all this was in vain. Before the troops arrived the hut, in which the Guru's body had been placed, was a huge pillar of fire. The gallantry displayed by Bhai Jaita, afterwards Jeewan Singh, was duly rewarded. Later he performed still greater deeds and won a name for all time.

According to another account which, in part, agrees with that of the author of Sair-ul-Mutakhirin Aurangzebe had ordered that the Guru's body be cut into four quarters and exposed at the four gates of the town. To avoid this ignominious treatment

Bhai Jaita suggested to his father that the body be removed before Aurangzebe's men should come to take it. It was, however, not an easy task to accomplish. The sentinels peeped into the cell every five minutes to satisfy themselves that all was right. Bhai Jaita proposed that he should die, the Guru's body be removed and his substituted in its stead. Parental affection refused consent. The father remonstrated urging that he, Bhai Jaita, was yet too young to die. At length, after much altercation, it was agreed that Jaita should cut his father's head and substitute the headless body with that of the Guru. The brave deed was accomplished unobserved to the eternal glory of both the father and the son.

After the Guru's obsequies were performed with due solemnity Govind Singh was formally installed on the *Gaddi* on the 1st Bisakh 1733 Vik, according to 1676 A. D. When the ceremonies in connection with the installation were over it was proposed to him that a campaign be organised to wreak vengeance on the tyrant Aurangzebe; but the proposal was not received with favour. He knew that his august father had himself sought his doom in order that by offering his life at the altar of his country he might set an example of self-sacrifice to the oppressed community to which he belonged and thereby create in them a feeling of resistance of authority deliberately misused in denationalising them and in forcing them to accept ways and beliefs in which they saw no beauty. He believed that his mission lay in nurturing and strengthening this feeling and in making his people self-respecting and self-reliant. So from this very time forward all his efforts were directed to bring about this result. Though young in years he was wise enough to see that all the ills from which the Hindu community suffered proceeded not from without but from within. Their own social fabric was not based on sound principles. Their religious convictions were not sufficiently strong. If relying solely on the Timeless One they performed their duties to themselves and to their country properly no external foe could dare do them harm. If, on the other hand, they were absorbed in compassing their individual ends and disregarded communal interests they must fall an easy prey into the hands of some foe or other. Therefore, he did not entertain proposals for war and commenced constructive work. The latter part of his life was spent on a war with the Moghals, no doubt ; but this war was entirely due to the intrigues and machinations of Raja Bhim Chand of Bilaspur, in the southern Himalyas, and other Rajas of the neighbouring hills who fell out with him for trivial reasons and whose whole resources were exhausted in endeavouring to destroy his growing influence, as would be shown later on.

He was then merely a lad. To undertake such a great task, at that age, would have been simply suicidal. He gave his whole time and attention to self-culture. He had in his pay dozens of eminent writers in verse who were attracted to his court from all places of learning and whom he employed in preparing vernacular editions of some of the choicest works in Sanskrit. Early at dawn he rose to perform ablutions and after reciting Japji and paying his regards to his mother and grandmother he attended the prayer meeting in the *Gurudwara* where his followers were already assembled and where after hearing the singing of hymns in praise of the Lord he recited a *Katha* from Granth Sahib and thereby satiated the craving of large congregations that daily came from the remotest regions of India and the North-West Frontier. This done he looked to the distribution of food to the visitors and to the poor. The rest of the day he spent at his palatial residence. If the weather was fine he went out for sport. His love for manly games necessitated the employment of many a brave spirit. The sons and grandsons of the warriors who had served under Guru Har Govind were sent for and entertained. Among them were some who subsequently earned great fame in Sikh history. In bad weather he stayed at home and satiated his intellectual appetites in select company. In the evening before it was dark he went to the *Gurudwara* and sat there late in the night. The programme of the morning was repeated. In addition to the Katha from the Ad Granth the hearers were entertained sometimes with recitations from Ramayana, Mahabharata and Hanuman Natak and sometimes with passages of his own composition.

All poets whose writings have influenced the destinies of nations were more or less inspired; but very few possessed Guru Govind Singh's power of expression. The force and pathos of his poetry, the purity of his style and the sublimity of purpose that underlies his writings are simply charming and to this day even if a poltroon hears them recited he is sure to be forthwith galvanised into action. It is this power of stirring up men's best feelings that, more than anything else, enabled him to wield such a vast influence over their hearts. And what is particularly noteworthy is that this power was utilised by him in elevating his followers and not in exciting their gross feelings to attain any unworthy object.

# CHAPTER IV.

Kabul, the Capital of Afghanistan, has always been noted for the manly bearing and large heartedness of its people. On a Besakhi festival Duni Chand, a trader from Kabul, presented the Guru with a woollen tent which surpassed in excellence even the one belonging to Emperor Aurangzebe. When it was erected in the *Maidan* the spectators were rooted to the ground in astonishment. They saw thereon, embroidered in gold and silver, representations of all that was grand and beautiful in nature. Men looked at the artistic work with feelings of great delight and ecstacy and admired Duni Chand and other disciples from Balkh, Bokhara and Kandhar on whose conjoint expense and labour the gift had been prepared. In the same year, on the occasion of the Diwali festival, Raja Rattan Rai of Assam came on a visit to the Guru. He was the son of Raja Ram Rai, an admirer of Guru Tegh Bahadur. Raja Ram Rai had no offspring and was consequently unhappy. Blessed by the Guru he got a son whom he named Rattan Rai. When he succeeded to the throne, Rattan Rai proposed to his mother that she should accompany him to Anandpur to pay respects to their benefactor's son. The mother very gladly expressed her willingness. So taking with them valuable presents and accompanied by a large retinue they started for Anandpur. On arrival there they were accommodated in the tent above-mentioned at the sight of which the Raja was lost in wonder and forgot the grandeur of his own court. Next day he brought as presents for the Guru an elephant named Pershadi with a forehead white as snow, and saddled with a seat wrought in gold, beautiful ponies, a curious weapon which when unfolded became by turns a spear, sword, gun and pistol, a sandal wood *chowki* with carved stands, a garland of pearls, a wig bedecked in precious stones and several *tháns* of Dacca Muslin. The presents were graciously accepted and the Raja was assigned a place of honour in the reception room. After making usual enquiries concerning the health of the royal visitor the Guru delivered a sermon on the various aspects of Dharma. The Guru's deep insight into the domain of religion astonished the Pandits who had accompanied the Raja and his heavenly beauty dazzled the Raja himself. The Raja's mother and Rani saw the Guru next day and received from him the solace of religion. All the while the Raja stayed with the Guru he was treated most kindly. He was regular in attending the divine service every morning and during the day he had the pleasure of accompanying the Guru's sporting parties. At length deeply impressed with all that he had seen and experienced the Raja left Anandpur for good. A temple was erected by him at the seat of his Government where to this day the Sikh visitors receive attention.

The order of Masands became a perfect scandal in the time of Guru Govind Singh. As agents of the Gurus the Masands were highly respected by the disciples in their respective spheres of work. To those who, for some reason or other, were unable to come and personally pay their respects to the Gurus they were as good objects of veneration as the Gurus themselves. The majority of the Masands succumbed to the many temptations to which they were exposed and made themselves obnoxious to the people. The disciples, simple as most of them were, could not muster courage enough to report to the Guru the nameless obscenities committed by the Masands. Once when the Guru was holding a Durbar, some itinerant dramatists availed themselves of an opportunity to bring the nefarious doings of his Masands to his notice. A person took the part of a Masand and another of a dancing girl. With two male attendants and riding on horseback the Masand and his paramour visited the house of a poor disciple. Finding the owner of the house absent he cursed him in a loud tone. The noise made attracted the disciple's wife to the door. On seeing the Masand she fell at his feet and asked for his blessings. She was rewarded with a kick and was asked to arrange for a number of beds. She brought the best ones in the house; but the Masand did not approve of them and flung them into the street. The woman, then, borrowed better beds from a neighbour. This done the Masand ordered one of the young daughters of the Sikh disciple to shampoo the dancing girl and sent the other after her father. His servants took as much of hay and fodder for the horses as they pleased; but when *Nehari* (a mixed food composed of gram flour, raw sugar and red pepper) was not forthcoming the wrath of the Masand knew no bounds. He was about to give the mistress of the house a beating when her husband returning from work fell at the man's feet and, as usual, prayed for his blessings. But poor as he was he failed to salute the Masand with a silver coin in his hand. This, coupled with his wife's incapacity to provide *Nehari* for the ponies, redoubled the Masand's anger. In fear, the man mortgaged his wife's ornaments and purchased provisions to serve dainty dishes to the Masand and his paramour. But as these did not include meat and liquor they were thrown to the dogs. At length the faithful disciple mortgaged a plot of his land and, with the money thus obtained, he provided such articles of food as he was asked to do and made presents of money and clothes to the Masand and his paramour, as well as to their male attendants. Next morning when the Masand prepared to leave he asked for the hand of one of the disciple's daughters for an attendant; but as she was already betrothed the Sikh was not able to comply with the demand. For this refusal he was rewarded with a shower of imprecations. The poor matron wept in distress and wished they had been rich enough to satisfy their guests and deserve better treatment at their hands. Her husband remarked that the Masand was the Guru's representative and, therefore, what he said and did ought to result in lasting good to them.

The Guru was already sick of the Masands. The heinous picture drawn before him drew forth tears from his eyes. He dismissed the performers laden with presents and thanked them for their enabling him to come to a decision on a matter of such serious moment. The messengers, sent throughout the country, brought the Masands bound in chains. They were tried and punished according to their deserts. Some were flogged; others were made to return their ill-gotten wealth to the owners; while the few who were found innocent were released and sent back rewarded. The order of Masands, however, ceased to exist from that date. The Sikhs were, thenceforward, forbidden to hold any intercourse with them.

# CHAPTER V.

The state of Hinduism in the time of Guru Govind Singh was as bad as can possibly be conceived. In Chapter III the measures that the Moghal Governors had taken to suppress Hinduism throughout Hindustan have been described at some length. But the Punjab, being Hindustan's gate through which all invaders, great and small, passed on their way to Delhi, had been receiving the brunt of the Muslim invasions for centuries previous. It was, therefore, constantly in an unsettled condition. The amenities of a regular Government, even of a tyrannical one, were not within the reach of the people. The places of worship of the Hindus were razed to the ground. To build new ones was a criminal act.

Those were the days of rank superstition and awful ignorance. As during the Dark Ages the whole Christendom was led to believe that seats in Heaven could be purchased through the intervention of the Popes, the Hindus were taught to give all they had to the Brahmans and seek death to reach Heaven earlier. An infernal machine, called *Kalwatra*, was erected in Benares. Thousands of pilgrims were sawn into pieces and their belongings were appropriated by the crafty priests. To sit in the midst of heaps of fire, to stand for weeks and months in cold water, breast deep, to lie down on iron nails and to cause bodily pain to one's self by similar devices, to burn alive women on the pyres of their husbands, to offer human sacrifices at the altar of the so-called deities and many other barbarous practices were regarded acts of merit. Thus the benighted humanity was murdered, robbed and plundered by its own priests. Here and there Hindu and Sikh Sadhus and learned Pandits inculcated higher ideas; but as such instances were rare they did no lasting good.

Apart from this the observance of caste rules had killed fellow-feeling from the minds of the Hindus and had made them cruel to and suspicious of one another.

The Sikhs in those days differed from the Hindus only in doctrinal matters mostly. In every other respect they were undistinguishable from the Hindus in thought and deed. The teachings of the previous nine Gurus had, no doubt, made them devont, more or less, but the inelastic Hindu social code still swayed them and forbade their existence as an independent community with power to frame laws for their own harmonious development. They still believed in Hindu Avatars and mythological heroes. Still the Hindu superstitions and customs governed their daily lives. They readily permitted themselves to be involved in any brawl or fray in which the Hindus happened to be engaged rightly or wrongly. They were thoroughly and completely identified with the Hindus in all agitations against the ruling race. No wonder, then, that they should have equally suffered with their Hindu kinsmen from both internal and external troubles.

# CHAPTER VI.

Guru Govind Singh sought to organise his followers, who were scattered far and wide and who belonged to the various grades and castes of the Hindus, into a real brotherhood united by not only a community of beliefs but by that of other worldly interests. Mere singing of hymns and recitation of the scriptures did not satisfy him. He yearnt for the adoption of the means wherewith he could inspire his people with the feelings of love, manliness and sacrifice.

It was when he was engaged in such mental pursuits that the Pandit whose duty was to recite *Kathas* from Maha Bharata, while lecturing to the Sikhs, dwelt on the manifold advantages that resulted from the performance of 'Havan.' The mighty Kshatrya princes of yore, said he, owed their strength and valour to the performance of 'Havan.' From Rama and Lakshmana down to Bhim and Arjun all the great warriors were blessed by the goddess Kali, invoked during the performance of this ceremony. The Guru had no faith in such superstitions; but pressed by a number of disciples and particularly to show the absurdity of the notion he gave his consent to the performance of the ceremony. Preparations were elaborate and expenditure profuse. Days, weeks and months passed, but the goddess did not appear. Some ingenious reply or other was given to the Guru's impatient enquiries. At length the cunning old priest, Kesho Das, who presided at the ceremony declared that the goddess would not appear unless the Guru sacrificed some sacred person at her altar. The Guru understanding what was passing in the man's mind observed that so far as he could think the presiding priest himself was the only person qualified to receive the distinction suggested. The night following the Pundit took all that he could and fled for his life. The Guru, thereupon, threw the whole *samigri* (ingredients) of 'Havan' into the fire. The night was pitch dark. The flames rose high and their fragrance pervaded the whole atmosphere. People on the distant hills ascribed this unusual illumination to the appearance of the goddess. Large crowds poured into Anandpur to congratulate the Guru on the successful termination of the ceremony. No time was, however, lost in making the proper explanation and exposing the deceitful behaviour of the runaway priest.

By this time a complete change came on the Guru. He was no more a jolly, communicative, dashing prince. His smiling face gave place to sadness and gloom. He shunned society and loved retirement. His admirers were filled with a feeling of alarm. The Masands who inwardly disliked him for the reprimands they had so often received rejoiced at the change which they thought would soon lead to insanity. But the Providence had decreed otherwise. The patient, if so he may be called, was, all this while, in communion with the Creator. He was suffering from an acute pain at the sight of so many of his countrymen and countrywomen sunk in deep ignorance and reduced to slavery. He prostrated himself before the Father Almighty and prayed for grant of power wherewith he could put life into his people. The prayer was heard. A voice from on high told him that he had been anointed as God's son and commissioned to save humanity from sin and suffering. Thus strengthened by divine support he came out of his place of retirement and taking a naked sword in hand and addressing a large assembly of his followers he told them that this was the goddess that had appeared to him and enquired if any one was ready to sacrifice his life at its altar for the sake of the Guru and the community. All was quiet. Not one out of the thousands assembled responded to the call. Colour vanished from the cheeks of many. The call was repeated. This time there was a response. Daya Ram Khatri of Lahore stood up and offered his head. He was taken into the adjoining tent. Down came the sword. A body fell with a thud. Blood flowed in torrents. The whole assembly was speechless with horror. In a couple of minutes the Guru came out and demanded another sacrifice. Dharma Jat boldly came forward and offered himself to be sacrificed. He, too, was taken inside. The sound of the sword, as it was brandished in the air, and the thud were again heard from the tent and blood flowed out in larger quantities. Struck with terror the Masands ran to the Guru's private residence and reported to mother Gujri that her son had actually become mad, that he was killing his disciples by his own hand and that if she did not interfere in time there was no knowing how many more lives would be lost. The good lady was naturally pained to hear all this; but, before her messengers arrived, to find out what the matter was, three more brave men Himmat, water carrier, Sahiba, barber, and Mohkam, washerman, had offered themselves to be sacrificed and had been treated like Daya Ram and Dharma. A few minutes more elapsed. The five brave men stood in new attire before their bewildered brethren. The Guru followed and seated the Five *Pyaras* (five loved ones) as thenceforward they were destined to be remembered in Sikh history, on the dais alongside of himself. He congratulated the assembled Sikhs on their possessing such brave souled men. He was sure that these five were not the only gems they possessed. When so many were ready to give away their very lives for the sake of *dharma* Sikhism was a real force destined to work wonders. They saw that instead of taking the lives of the Five *Pyaras* he had killed goats. He had resorted to this procedure to know if his people were ready to give their lives at his bidding. The device had succeeded to his immense satisfaction.

The disciples now gave free vent to their long pent up feelings and the air resounded with the cries of " Sat Sri Akal! " (The Timeless One is true!) Some regretted that they should have failed in offering their lives and earning this unique honour. Others were glad that the awful scene they had witnessed a few moments previous was at last over. In this way the evening passed off pleasantly.

# CHAPTER—VII

The morning after the incidents related at the close of the last chapter, *i.e.*, on the 1st of Baisakh, Samvat 1756 Vik., according to 1699 A. D., the disciples mustered in force on the terrace of Kesgarh, in response to an invitation. Dressed in pure white the Guru came and seated himself on the throne. The Five *Pyaras* were sent for and marshalled in front of the Guru. They were asked to pronounce Wah-i-Guru! (Hail the Divine Teacher!), Wah-i-Guru!, Wah-i-Guru!, in audible tones and to fix their minds on the Lord. An iron bowl was sent for and some water and sugar were put into it. The Guru stirred the water, thus mixed, with the point of the two edged dagger he held in his right hand. All this while to sanctify the water he recited hymns in praise of the Lord of Hosts.

This the water was converted into *Amrita*, the water that when drunk made immortals of the mortals. It was then, by turns, administered to the Five *Pyaras* who were thereupon made to shout aloud "Wah-i-Guru ji ka Khalsa, Sri Wah-i-Guru ji ki fateh!" (The Khalsa is of the Divine Teacher! Victory is of the Divine Teacher!) They were further required to recite some hymns in praise of the Lord and then they all partook of *Karah Parshad* (a cooked food composed of equal quantities of sugar, flour and *ghee* and as much water) from the same vessel to show that they renounced caste prejudices, so far as these affected inter-dining. The Guru bade them to remember that thenceforward they were all brothers and members of one church called *Khalsa* (unalloyed, pure). They were to regard him as their spiritual father and his wife Sahib Devi as their mother. They were to preach the brotherhood of man and were to believe in one God alone. They were all to assume the name of 'Singh' (lion) and to carry arms on their person. They were to wear garments suited to the life of a soldier. They were to abhor tobacco and other intoxicants in any form. They were to stand by one another in time of trouble and lastly in all that they did they were to be fair and upright. The Guru then drank *Amrita* from the same vessel and partook of *Karah Parshad* offered by the Five *Pyaras*.

The baptism of the spirit and the sword thus administered inaugurated a new era in the history of Indian reform. Before Guru Govind Singh not one person of such a high descent and standing had taken such a bold step and faced the consequent risks. With one stroke the illustrious Guru did away with distinctions that had engendered selfishness and man-hatred and had made spiritual and political slaves of the Hindus. The new community with such beliefs and aspirations led by a person so august and brave started on its career. Men belonging to the lowest orders of the Hindu society and treated as helots in Greece and Plebeans in Rome, became great leaders and brave warriors. Peasants, hitherto never mentioned in history and kept in ignorance deliberately, became preachers of the new Gospel and boldly entered into discussions with the advocates of the old, dead and dying beliefs Not unlike the English Puritans their simple ideas, simple garb, pure lives and sincere regard and earnestness for the establishment of the reign of virtue won them universal admiration. Their very contact, nay the very sight of them served as a spell. In spite of themselves men felt a strong craving to be admitted into the new *Panth* (fold). In a word, "the hitherto neglected and down-trodden humanity all of a sudden was roused into activity. It became conscious of its strength and eagerly sought for opportunities to display it." The votaries of the new creed worked, lived and died for what they considered to be good and honourable. Straightforward, outspoken, guileless and confiding, staunch friends of the weak and the defenceless and implacable foes of the strong and the oppressive they were respected and feared wherever they went and wherever they lived. They were no longer quiet, timid, hymn singing devotees with little tambition and still less spirit. They no longer submited passively to the vain, selfish and privileged classes that had kept them down from time immemorial and had made them "hewers of wood and drawers of water." They no longer looked with respect on the Shastras that had made it criminal for them to aspire for things higher. Their souls freed from the thraldom of ages, their eyes opened, their minds widened, they vigorously turned their attention to the exposure of fall false pretences and all injustice in religion, politics and social autonomy. The authority of the priestly classes and their adherents among Rajputs and Kshatryas was defied and, taught by a leader who though so high, loved to be regarded as one of them, they learnt that they were God's soldiers sent down to protect his kingdom and punish his enemies.

# CHAPTER VIII.

Guru Govind Singh taught belief in one great God, "the Timeless one," as he called Him. According to him God is Just, Merciful, All-Powerful, Omniscient and All-Loving. He does not take birth as Hindus and Christians believe. Considering that Hindus were too much prone to regard their great men as incarnations of the Deity and that his followers who mostly came from that stock might not fall into this error he told them in the clearest possible language that those who would call him God would be thrown into hell. Enjoins he:—

"Bin Kartár na kirtam máno,
Ád ajon ajai abnáshi teh Parmeshar jáno,
Káha bhaiyo jo án jagat meṇ dasak Asur Har ghác;
Adhak parpaṇch dikháe sabhan kah ápe Brahm kaháe.
Bhaṇjan, gharaṇ samrath sadá Prabhu so kim ját gináyo,
Táṇte sarb kál ko asko gháe bacháe na áyo,
Kaise tohe tár hai sun jaṛ áp dubyo bhau ságar,
Chhúṭ ho kál pháṇs te tab hí gao saru jagatágar."

The Creator and not created objects should be worshipped. He alone should be considered *Parmeshar* who is the Primeval Being, never takes birth, is unconquerable and indestructible. What if *Har* came into this world, killed some ten *Asurs* (aborigines) exhibited lots of puzzling feats and finally himself posed as God? The eternal Lord Himself has power to make and to destroy. Why should he have permitted himself to be regarded as belonging to a particular caste? The pretender after divine honours was not able to save himself from the blow struck by the Angel of Death. How can he take across any one who himself was drowned in the Sea of Fear? Those who desire to escape from the noose of death should take shelter with the Lord of the Universe." Numerous such passages are extant over his writings which all tend to show unmistakably that Guru Govind Singh did not believe in the theory of God's incarnation.

He was not a worshipper of images. On the contrary he openly condemned image worship. Says he :—

Káhú lai páhan púj dhario sir káhú lai ling gare latkáyo,
Káhú lakhyo Har awáchí dishá men, káhú pachháh ko sís niwáyo,
Káhú bután ko pújat hai pasu káhú mritán ko púj n dháyo,
Kúr kriyá urjhyo sabhí jag Sri Bhagwán ko bhed na páyo.

"Some people take idols and reverentially place them on their heads. Some wear the *Lingam* round their necks. Some search for God towards the east, some bow their heads towards the west. Some benighted people worship images, some adore tombs. The whole world is entangled in false pursuits. The secret of *Sri Bhagwan* no one has found out."

Though he respected all great men and valued all good work he did not put faith in the so-called revealed books. Says he :—

Páe gahe jab te tumre tabte koú áńkh tare nahin ányon,
Ráma, Rahím, Puráua, Qurán, anek kahain mat ek na mányon,
Simrita, Shastra, Bed sabai baoh bhed kahen ham ek na jányon,
Bed, Purán, Kateb, Qurán abhed nirpáu sabhai pach háre,
Bhed na pái sakyo Anbhed ko khedat hai Anchhed pukáre.

Rág, na rúp na rekh na rang na sák na sog na sang tehúre.
Ád, Anád, Agádh, Abhekh, Adwaikh japyo tin hí kul táre......
Bed kateb bikhe Har náhin.
Ján leho Har jan man máhin.

"Since I have taken shelter at Thy feet O, Lord !, I have noticed no one. Rama, Rahim, the Puranas, Quran, talk of numerous faiths; I acknowledge not even one of them. The Smritis, the Shastras, the Vedas all teach contradictions; I believe not in any of them.........The Vedas, the Puranas, the Books, the Quran and sovereign princes have failed to know Thy mystery. They have not been able to fathom the depth of Thou Unfathomable One. They call Thee Untraceable while toiling after Thee. Thou hast no attachments, no features, no lineaments, no colour, no sorrow and no associate. Generations of those have attained salvation who meditate on Thee, the First One, the Eternal, the Unknowable and The One above rancour and prejudice.........Understand ye believers Hari is not in the Vedas and the Books: He is enshrined in your own hearts."

In pre-British period and chiefly when the Brahmans were in ascendancy people were taught to attach too much importance to *Pranayam* and to various forms of austerities.

Guru Govind Singh emphatically condemned these practices. Says he :—

Ankh múnd koú dimbh dikháwai,
Andhar kí padwí kah páwai,
Ankh mích mag sújh na jái,
Táhi Anant mile kim Bhái,
Je je bhekh sutan men dhúre
Te Prabhu jan kuchh kái na bicháre,

Samajh liyo sab jan man máhiṇ,
Dhimban meṇ Parmeshar náhíṇ.
Je je karam kar dimbh dikháí.
Tin Prabh logan meṇ gat náhíṇ.
Jíwat chalat jagat ke kájá,
Swáṇg dekh kar pújat Rájá,
Swângan men Parmeshar náhíṇ,
Khoj phirai sabhí ko káhíṇ,
Apno man kar mo jih áná.
Pár Brahma ko tiní pachháná.
Bhekh dikháe jagat ko logan ko bas kín,
Aṇt kál kátí katyo bás narak moṇ lín,
Násá múṇd karai parnáma.
Phokat dharm na kaudí káma,
Háth hiláe surg na jáú,
Je man jít saká na káú.

"He who pretends sanctity by closing his eyes shall attain the position of the bat. By closed eyes one can not feel his way. How, then, can the Endless One be seen by so doing? God's people do not attach any value to those who appear in the various garbs of saintliness. Understand ye people God can not be obtained by resorting to hypocritical ways. Those who act hypocritically are not respected by godly men. As long as such persons live, their worldly objects are gained; for kings and princes, deceived by appearances, worship such persons; but God can not be seen in men who pose as His representatives; though all may search for them anywhere. Those alone know God who control their minds. Those who wear saintly garbs and enslave mankind will be cut by the knife and thrown into hell. The belief of those who close their nostrils and perform *Pranayam* is false and worth not a shell. The moving of hands will take none to heaven unless passions are subdued." In another place says he :—

Na jatá múṇd dhároṇ, na mundraká swároṇ,
Japo tás náma sarai sarb káma,
Na nainaṇ micháúṇ na dhimbhaṇ dikháúṇ,
Na kukaram kamáúṇ na bhekhí kaháúṇ.

"I wear not matted hair on my head. I do not adorn my ears with ear-rings. I repeat the name of the One who assists in all things. I sit not with eyes half closed. I deceive no one. No evil deed do I perform, no spurious garb do I wear."

To escape from sin and suffering and thus to attain to salvation he pointed out an easy way, *viz.*, repeating the name of the Lord. Says he :—

Jin jin nám tiháró dhiáyá,
Dúkh páp tin nikat na áyá,
Bin Har nám na báchan pai hai,
Chaudah lok jáhe bas kíne tá te káhe palai hai,
Rámá, Rahim, ubhár na sak hai, jáṇ kah nám ratai hai.
Brahma, Bishan, Rudra, Surya, Sassya te bas kál sabai hai.
Beda, Purana, Quran, sabhai mat já kah net kahai hai.
Indra, Phanindra, Munindra Kalap baho dhiyáwat dhiyán na ai hai.
Ja kah rúp rang na jánivat so kim Syáma kahai hai,
Chhutho kál phás te tábhí táhe charnan liptai hai.

"Those that meditate on Thy name sin and suffering approach not." "Without the Lord's name salvation is impossible. How canst thou, O man, hide thyself from what (Death) has subdued the four een worlds? Rama and Rahim whose names thou epeatest can not raise thee. (Have they not all become victims of Death? Come and take shelter with the Lord of Lords before whom the mightiest of the mighty bow their heads in submission.) Brahma, Vishnu, Rudra, Surya, Sasya, all are in the clutches of Death. Whom the Vedas, the Puranas, the Quran, all call Eternal, whom Indra, Phanindra, Manindra, have for ages meditated on and of whom they have failed to form a conception, whose features and colour no one knows, why dost thou benighted man call Him Syama (dark-coloured)? Then alone wilt thou be disentangled from the noose of Death when thou clingest thyself to the feet of the Eternal One."

Guru Govind Singh belonged to the class of great men who, though they boldly preached their ideas and even suffered death for upholding them, resented the application of force in matters of belief. Like the Vedantis and Sufis of the higher type he saw God in all things and considered it a sacrilege to look down on any human being, however humble or low-placed.

Maulana Rum, the famous Sufi, whose name will live for all time in the religious history of the world says:—

Nest áṇ jáe ki áṇjá jalwa-i-jánánáṇ nest.
Chíst andar Ka'ba hairánam ki dar but khánǽ nest.
Aftáb-i-yak diyáro gauhar-i-yak ma'danem.
Ashnáyánem bá ham hech kas begáná nest.

"There is no place where the lustre of the Loved One is not. What is there in Ka'aba, I wonder, which is not in a Pagoda? We are the sun of the same heaven and jewels of the same mine. We are all mutual friends not one is a stranger." The gospel of love preached by this great saint was not acceptable to the *Ulemas* of the community to which he was connected by the mere accident of birth and which had flourished mainly by the application of force. For his outspoken advocacy of the principle of toleration in matters of belief the Moulana was hounded to death. Guru Govind Singh preached the same principle and received the same treatment from the people in whose interest he worked all his life. Says he:—

> Koú bhaiyo múndya Sanyásí.
>
> Koú Jogí bhai Brahmachárí Koú Jatian mánbo,
>
> Hindu, Turk, koú Ráfzí, Imámsháfí, máunsh kí ját sabhai ek paichánbo,
>
> Kartá Karím sohí, Rázik Rahím ohí, dúsrá na bhed koí bhúl bhram mánbo.
>
> Delhrá Masít sohí Pújá au namáj ohí, mánush sabhai ek hai anek ko prabháo hai.
>
> Dewatá, Adew, Jachha, Gáhndharva, Turk, Hindú, niáre, niáre desan ke bhes ko prabháo hai,
>
> Ek ek hí sarup sabai ekai jot jánbo.

"Some are Udasis, Sanyasis, some are Yogis, some Brahmacharis: some call themselves Jatis, some call themselves Hindus, some Turks, some Rafzis and Imam Shafis. Believe all mankind as one. Karta and Karim are the same; Raziq and Rahim the same: entertain not the least doubt about it even mistakenly." "Temple and Masjid are the same; "Puja" and "Namaz" the same; men are all of one essence; though they appear different. Devatas, Asurs, Yakshyas, Gandharvas, Turks and Hindus are so called on account of local considerations of different climes and countries. They are all brothers and are all equally the emanations of the Great Spirit that enlivens all."

He scouted the idea of this or that race being the chosen people of God, or that there was anything inherent in any class of men that made them incapable of aspiring after higher life. He condemned with great force the practice of making God responsible for the various so called holy wars that were waged to enslave or exterminate weaker races. On no point he has laid so much stress in his writings as on the all-loving nature of God. Says he :—

Rogan te ar sogan te jal jogan te bauh bhánt bachánwai,
Satru anek chalawai ghaw tau tan ek na lágau páwai,
Rákhat hai apno kar de kar páp sabhuhan bhet na páwai.

"The Heavenly Father protects from sickness and sorrow, and from sea monsters in many ways. Numerous foes are always lying in wait to strike thee, o, man; but thou receivest not one blow! He extends thee His helping hand and all malevolent influences approach thee not."

# CHAPTER IX.

The new creed was named "Khalsa Panth" (pure way). The persons baptised were called Khalsas (pure ones). According to the Guru "the man who meditates day and night on the Ever Shining Light and does not give place in his heart to any one except the One; who adorns himself with the belief in the love of the Perfect One; who discards fasts and tomb worship; who in alms-giving, commisseration, asceticism and continence recognises not any other save the One; in whose heart burns the light of the Perfect One alone deserves to be known as a true Khalsa."

The baptism of the spirit and the sword did produce such men. Possessed of an iron-will the baptised easily conquered their passions and thus acquiring supremacy over the enemy within them they became conquerors of the world outside. In response to a proclamation issued by the Guru multitudes of people came to Anandpur to receive baptism and parties of the disciples were sent all round the country to spread the new Gospel.

These itinerant preachers met with considerable success and not many years elapsed before a band of earnest men gathered round the banner of the new creed.

The rise of the new creed, however, failed to elicit a feeling of gratitude or even of admiration from the breasts of high caste people generally. On the contrary it provoked hostility in all conservative centres. For a time this opposition was not a pronounced one; but in proportion as the number of converts to the new Gospel increased their open disregard of old beliefs and rituals engendered a bitterness which soon assumed a serious form. People forgot the blessings they had received from the Sikh Dispensation. The purity and soundess of its basal principles was ignored. They regarded the new doctrines as heresies and thought it an act of merit to do all they could to prevent their getting hold over men's minds. But as has been the case everywhere the opposition of the conservative element strengthened still more the hearts of the reformers and bound them more closely together. The mere sight of a Sikh gladdened another Sikh. A Sikh way-farer finding a co-religionist lying wearied and exhausted on the roadside at once laid down his things, shampooed the man and shared with him the loaf of bread or roasted corn that he carried with him for his own use. In a word, the Sikhs of those times shared their sorrows and pleasures with one another and as they were devoutly religious, sacrificing and confiding, they were able to take united action in many a concern of life.

Special festivals were organised which were largely attended. Men came from distant lands to meet in "a common worship and share in a common amusement," and just as these great national gatherings were of peculiar importance in Grecian history they played not a small part in the history of Sikh progress. In the words of a European historian they were of great use in "fostering a common national pride, a sound physical training, intellectual vigour and emulation and a healthy desire for success in every kind of competition, where the reward consisted chiefly in the high opinions won from their fel-

At this time the Raja of Bilaspur visited Anandpur accompanied by several other hill chieftains. The Guru received them in an open Durbar and in an eloquent speech asked them and other high-caste Hindu leaders, assembled on the occasion, to join hands with him in his campaign of reform. "Their ancestors" said he, "were the Lord's Paramount in the country. They made and administered laws according to their requirements. From time immemorial they were accustomed to receive homage from contemporary potentates and men of note and influence. Their people were happy and prosperous. In religion, as in arts, nations of the world considered it a privilege to follow their lead. But the state of things had, then, undergone a complete change. They were no more a self-governing, conscientious and sacrificing people. Their religion was discarded. Their places of worship were insulted and demolished. Their men were taken into slavery. Their women were forcibly removed into the seraglios of the Turks and their children were sold in the market of Kabul and Kandhar for a penny a head. They were no more masters but slaves in their own land, incapable of doing a good turn to themselves or to others. What was this due to? Certainly the land had not changed; neither the elements had grown fickle in their ministration of beneficence. The same Himalayas fed the streams that watered their fields and gardens and quenched their thirst. The same lands yielded them numerous varieties of corn and luscious fruits. The same sun and air refreshed their souls and purified their homes. Thousand and one other blessings existed as of yore. Evidently, therefore, the fault was their's and their's alone. They had ceased worshipping God Almighty and had taken to the worship of stocks and stones instead. This had deprived them of the only source of goodness and had consequently destroyed fellow-feeling in their minds. Their religion was only an hallucination, their social system was still worse. It was based on selfish principles that brought good to few and evil to many. Professedly intended to bind people into one homogeneous whole, in reality it engendered and nurtured man-hatred. Did they not daily witness the sight of large crowds of Hindus overawed by a handful of the conquering race? And did they not notice that the members of this race were powerful because their hearts were united, while they, the Hindus, would not suffer for one another's troubles? If they still desired to have a place among the living and progressive nations of the world, he would ask them to enter the fold of the Khalsa Panth and be saved from the otherwise inevitable downfall and extinction."

This pathetic appeal failed to move the stone-hearted hill-men, in whom all manliness had become dead. "The Guru," they replied, "being gifted with miraculous powers could well afford to face the mighty Moghul. He was, moreover, a Faqir having no land or country of his own. Wherever he lived was his home. This was not the case with them. They were men of the world having much to lose. The Moghuls would not notice him seriously; for they knew they could not wrest from him any territory or treasure. But what would be their position? They would be kicked and turned out from the land of their fathers and would be either killed or sold as slaves. They knew full well the might of the Moghuls and regarded the expectations raised by the new agitation as mere idle dreams. The religious and social propaganda of the Guru was still less acceptable to them. They refused to believe that any ceremony could drive out the brute from the base-born or that any good could come out of promiscuous eating and inter-mingling with the low castes who formed the major portion of his followers. They saw no harm in the worship of idols, and they did not see why they should not stick to their old ways and beliefs. They had come to Anandpur out of mere curiousity to see how the low castes looked in their new garb. The previous nine Gurus had confined themselves to the preaching of God's name and impressing upon the people the importance of Bhakti (devoutness) above all other things. They did not disturb the old order of things or introduce any revolutionary measure. They wished to be understood that these changes were not acceptable to them."

Ghulam Mohi-ud-din, a contemporary Muslim historian, thus refers to the above address of the Guru and to the response with which it was met:—

Hama há dar yak mazhab dar áyand ki dúí az darmiyán bar khezad wa har chahár warn i Hanúd az Bráhman, wa Kshatrya wa Súdra wa Vaish ki har yak rá dar Dharm Shastra dín i alaihda muqarar ast ánrá tark dáda bar yak tarík salúk numáyand, wa hama barábar and wa yake khud rá bar dígare tarjíh na dihad wa tírath hái manind i Gang wagaira ánki dar Ved Shástar t'alim i ánhá tákíd i mazíd rafta ast az khátar badar kunand wa sawái az Gurú Nának wa khuláfái o bar dígar az sanádíd i Hanúd masal Rám, Kishan, wa Brahmá wa Dewí wagairá i'tiqád na namaiyand. Wa Pahul i man girifta marduman i har chahár baran dar yak zaraf bikhurand, wa az yak digár islah burand. Ham chunín sukhnan bisyár guftand. Chún marduman bishinidand bisyáre az Bráhmanán wa Chhatriyán barkhástand wa guftand ki mazhabé ki mukhálif i Ved Shástar bawad hargiz qabúl namé kunéin wa mazhab i kuhna ki péshínigan barán iqdám namúdand ba guftai kodaké (Guru Gobind Singh was a young man then) az dast na dihém. Ín gufta bar khástand. Magar bist hazár kas razá dádand wa mutábaqat bar zubán áwurdand.

"That all should come into (the fold of) one religion, so that the difference between them (the Hindus and the men of the new Faith) may disappear and all the four castes of the Hindus, *viz.*, the Brahmans, the Chhatris, the Vaishas, and the Shudras, for each of which the Ved Shastra has prescribed a different creed, may leave that creed and deal with one another according to one creed; that they should consider each other as equals and no one should think himself superior to another. And all pilgrimages like that to the Ganges, etc., which are enjoined in the Vedas and Shastras must be removed from the mind and with the exception of Guru Nanak and his successors, none like Rama, Krishna, Brahma and Devi, &c., should be believed in. And after taking my *Pahul* (baptism), men of all the four castes may eat out of one vessel and may learn from one another. He (Guru Gobind Singh) said a great many things like this. When the people heard them, many of the Brahmans and Chhatris got up and said that they would never accept a creed that was opposed to the Vedas and Shastras and they would not give up the old religion which their ancestors had believed in, upon the advice of a youth (Guru Gobind Singh was a young man then). Saying this they got up; but twenty thousand people accepted the propaganda and agreed to act up to its principles."

The Guru, finding it useless to argue any further with men who were mentally so low, changed the topic of the discourse and turned to the monstrous gathering of the disciples to whom his mere look was life and his mere word law and in an impressive sermon prepared them for the coming struggle. Little did the hill Rajputs who boasted their high lineage think that the time was not very distant when the very same low-caste Jats, whom they so openly discarded and for reclaiming whom they harboured sinister motives against the Guru, would shed their blood to chastise their Moslem oppressors, would rescue their men and women from infamy, and would make the desecration of their temples and the breaking of their idols a thing of the past! Little did they know that not a century would elapse before these low-castes would rule over them; nay would even employ them as their gate-keepers and orderlies.

One day when the Guru went out for *shikar* he bagged a large tiger. An ass was dressed in the skin of this tiger and let free to roam about in the fields. For several days the ass freely grazed in the extensive farms and grew fat. The farmers believing him to be a real tiger dared not go near him. Once in the course of his wanderings the ass thought of paying a visit to the house of his master who was a washerman. It was twilight. Men were returning to their homes after the day's work. Shops and places of business were about to be closed. The sight of the ass, in the tiger's garb, as he sauntered along the streets, inspired terror in the minds of the people who fled for their lives in all directions. The ass, however, took no notice of the agitation his presence in the village had caused and went straight to the washerman's house. The women and children of the house ran upstairs and shrieked for help. Meantime the washerman returned from work. He, too, was at first alarmed on seeing the brute; but noticing that the animal quietly grazed he felt emboldened to go a little nearer. On seeing his old master the ass brayed in way of recognition. Forthwith the washerman took a club and gave him a good beating. "Vicious brute," said he, "why and where didst thou keep away so long? I see thou hast grown fat. I shall place double load on thee henceforth." When it was made known in the village that the brute that had caused so much fright to the entire population was only an ass there was great uproar and laughter. People cursed themselves for having been so easily befooled and many were the men who regretted that they should have failed to approach the brute and administer him kicks to their heart's satisfaction. Next morning the Guru related the last night's incident to the disciples in the audience hall. The moral of the story, said he, was evident. So long as the ass kept aloof from his past company the tiger's skin protected him from insults and enabled him to graze unmolested wherever it so pleased him. He was, further, feared by both man and beast who all fled at the very sight of him. But he was, after all, an ass. The tiger's skin aided him temporarily but could not make a veritable tiger of him. Similarly those who assumed Sikh forms without imbibing Sikh spirit resembled the donkey with the tiger's skin. They might, for a time, deceive people and obtain temporary distinction ; but their exposure was inevitable, sooner or later, and they would not fare better than the donkey of the story.

As is the case nowadays, in the Guru's time, too, there were lots of black sheep in the fold. The continued stay of the Guru at Anandpur had attracted a large number of disciples from places near and remote. The more wealthy of the disciples established *langars* (free kitchens) from where the poor and the needy could get food. This free distribution of food was considered an act of merit and those who performed it won popular esteem. Some of the Guru's agents and courtiers who traded in the name of religion and whose business was to deal with the visitors in their respective countries considered it incumbent on them to start *langars* of their own. But most of what they did was mere show. One night the Guru, dressed as a Sadhu, went round the town and asked for food from all the *langars*. Nobody recognised him. In most places his request for food was refused. Some gave him stale and dried crumbs of bread on the plea that the fresh food had been used up. Only from the *Langars* of Diwan Nand Chand, Bhais Nand Lal, Ram Kaur and Sahib Chand fresh and sufficient food was obtained. The following day the Guru related the experience of the night and exhibited the crumbs of bread. This public exposure of men who pretended virtue had a salutary effect on the morals of the Sikhs.

# CHAPTER X.

The Guru's teachings were a menace to the power of the hill Rajas. Such despots have yet to be born who would allow in their own territories the holding of conferences where men are taught to challenge the birth right of priests and princes and where the brotherhood of man is not only taught but practised. The sight of the Sikhs eating from the same *langar* (common kitchen), on the same *Chowka*, disregardful of the fact as to who cooked the food, who distributed it and who shared it with them exasperated the hill Rajputs who to this day are very conservative in such matters and who would not for any consideration allow men of lower castes to sit with them on the same couch. They regarded such practices as an attack on old customs and usages ; nay as preliminaries to an attack on their own authority as well.

At this time the number of immigrants into Anandpur increased considerably. Some of them were attracted by their love for sport, while the great majority consisted of the refugees whom Aurangzebe's persecution had made homeless. The Guru knew well that by according protection to such men he was giving Aurangzebe a cause for provocation ; but the laws of chivalry, that then obtained, and his position as a great spiritual leader, left him no other alternative. For his own and for their protection it was considered imperative to drill the few hundred attendants that he then had and to constantly remain prepared for an attack from outside. Thus a small standing corps was formed, the maintenance of which in a state of efficiency necessitated the adoption of military forms and usages. Whenever he went out for an excursion the men of this corps, of course, accompanied him. The beating of the drum, the martial array and the soldierly bearing of the party, excited jealousy in the breast of Bhim Chand, Raja of Bilaspur, in whose territory lay the estate of Anandpur. He sent word to the Guru to disband the corps or else he would turn him out of Anandpur. This threat was accompanied with a demand for Pershadi, the elephant presented by the Raja of Assam. The Guru refused to comply. Messengers after messengers came from the Raja to ask for the elephant; but as presents made by the disciples were inalienable the Guru stuck to his previous resolution. At length, advised by Pamma, his family priest, the Raja formally declared war against the Guru.

The news spread like fire. The veterans in the service of the Guru hailed the advent of an opportunity to win laurels in the field. But colour fled from the cheeks of the parasites who only knew to eat and drink and to live upon the offerings of the disciples. Fearing their occupation would be gone in case the Guru was defeated and driven out from Anandpur they waited upon his mother and grandmother and requested them to prevail upon him to yield. The ladies accordingly sent for the Guru and, in a very loving tone, asked him to give up his active propaganda and lead the life of an ascetic like most of his predecessors. They told him that for such freaks his grandfather, Guru Hargovind, had to leave

Amritsar and that if he, too, followed in his grandfather's footsteps they were afraid they would have to leave Anandpur too. Bhim Chand, as head of the princes who ruled over the southern Himalayas, would be a formidable opponent. Further, there was the danger of Aurangzebe's coming to help the Rajas, in which case it would be simply impossible for him to hold his ground. The Guru listened to the speech with respect ; but he submitted to the ladies in a decisive and firm tone, that his mission did not resemble that of his predecessors in the *Guddee* in all respects ; that times had changed and along with them had changed their requirements. His effort was to breathe a new spirit into his followers which would enable them to resist wrong-doers and to hold their own against all possible opponents. Instead of himself coming forward and taking the lead in the effort to afford such relief to the oppressed as was possible, Bhim Chand was placing every hindrance in the way of national upheaval ; for fear lest the reformers, if successful, might turn their eyes on his own principality. Jealous to the extreme, of a suspicious bent of mind and of wavering resolution, Bhim Chand was not a man to be trusted. Someday or other a trial of strength was to take place and the sooner it happened the better. He was, therefore, not prepared to yield to the threats of the wily hill chieftain.

War was, however, avoided. The betrothal ceremony of Ajmere Chand, Bhim Chand's son, being at hand, it was thought inauspicious to inaugurate it by bloodshed.

# CHAPTER XI.

No son having been born of Jeetoji, the Guru's first wife, his mother and grand-mother insisted on his second marriage. So in 1684 A.D. the Guru was married to Sundri Devi, daughter of Ram Saran, Kumrao Khatri of Bijwara. Prince Ajit Singh was the offspring of this union.

In those days the Guru settled a long standing boundary dispute between Raja Maidni Prakash of Nahan and Raja Fateh Shah of Srinagar, Gharwal. This gave rise to the growth of a feeling of cordiality between these two Chiefs and the Guru. The Raja of Nahan offered him a vast estate and so deeply attached he became to him that he insisted on his residing there permanently. The Guru found it difficult to wholly refuse an offer so kindly made. He consented to live in the Nahan Territory, as long as circumstances permitted, and accordingly in the month of Magh the foundations of the fortress of Paunta were laid at a picturesque spot on the banks of Jamna. The fortress was soon completed and a separate mansion was built for the Guru's residence, the remains of which exist to this day. Here the Guru resided for a couple of years. Raja Fateh Shah and Raja Maidni Prakash were his constant visitors and they frequently accompanied his *shikar* parties.

From a long time previous Sodhi Ram Rai had settled himself in the territory of Raja Fateh Shah and had made a large following there. He had taken an active part in the proceedings that ultimately led to the death of Gurus Harkrishna and Tegh Bahadur.

On finding the increase of the Guru's influence over Fateh Shah and fearing lest this might prove prejudicial to him he sought for a reconciliation. In this attempt he was successful. A meeting was arranged at which the Sodhi was granted pardon and assurances were given to him of future protection and good will.

Budhu Shah, a Muhammadan saint of Sadhaura, was, in those days, touring in that region. Hearing of the Guru's renown he came to pay his respects. The meeting was cordial and resulted in the establishment of life-long friendship.

Aurangzebe had, for some reason, dismissed five hundred Pathans whom no Hindu or Mussalman ruler dared to employ. On the recommendation of Budhu Shah and taking pity on their condition the Guru took them into his service. The Sirdars Kale Khan, Bikhan Khan, Najabat Khan, Hayat Khan and Umar Khan were paid Rs. 5 per day and the men a rupee a day.

# CHAPTER XII.

Guru Govind Singh was a great patron of learning. He had great love for the study of Sanskrit and was anxious that his people should know all that was good in the Shastras. Pundits, famous for their learning, were employed to render important Sanskrit works into vernacular and one Raghu Nath Pundit was engaged to teach Sanskrit to the Sikhs. When this Pundit came to know that among the pupils many were carpenters, Jats, washermen and barbers he refused to teach them. According to the Shastras, said he, the Sudras who read and the men who taught them Sanskrit were both guilty of a crime which required pouring of molten lead into their ears and though the Brahmans had long since lost political ascendancy and such punishment could not, therefore, be inflicted he was sure if he carried out the Guru's orders he would incur mortal hatred of his caste people. The Guru dismissed the Brahman immediately and sent five promising youths Karm Singh, Ganda Singh, Vir Singh, Saina Singh, and Ram Singh to Benares where assuming *Gairic* dress and adopting the life of Brahmacharis they acquired competency in Sanskrit lore. After a few years they returned and under the honoured title of *Nirmalas* (pure ones) they did great service in illumining men's minds.

In the year 1685 A. D. news was brought of the tragic end of Sodhi Ram Rai. He had incurred enmity of some of his corrupt Masands. On one occasion when he was absorbed in meditation they represented him to be dead and despite the protests of his wife, Punjab Kaur, cremated him alive. Punjab Kaur wrote to the Guru informing him of the true version of the affair and praying that he should come and put matters right. The dastardly behaviour of the Masands enraged every one, particularly the Guru, who immediately proceeded to Dehra Dun on a visit of condolence and assuring Punjab Kaur of sympathy returned to Paunta. In response to an invitation issued by Punjab Kaur the Masands of the late Sodhi came to Dehra Dun, on the 17th day of his death, to offer mourning gifts. The Guru, too, came accompanied by Diwan Nand Chand, his cousins Mohri and Sango, uncle Kirpal Chand, Durga Ji, Jawahir Ji, Bhikhan Khan, Kale Khan and other veterans. Punjab Kaur received every one with due respect. Next day the Guru reprimanded the Masands for their misbehaviour. Not a word of regret or penitence was heard. On the contrary he was confronted with the reply that being a guest he had no business to meddle with other people's affairs. Finding that not the proper time to take any action in regard to the matter the Guru kept quiet. *Dastarbandi* ceremony was then performed. His gifts to Punjab Kaur consisted of a garland of pearls, a bracelet of gold and a white shawl. Other kinsmen and friends made suitable presents. All the Masands assembled in a meeting, the day following, to receive *Khila'ts*. Bhai Sundar, Punjab Kaur's principal agent, desired them to shift to another room close by. About sixty soldiers had been already stationed at the entrance of that room. As each Masand entered he was subjected to a very searching examination. Those who were found to be innocent were released while the guilty were incarcerated in a room set apart for the purpose. Some were fined, others flogged, while a few were put to death. The news of this exemplary punishment had a salutary effect. Thenceforward the Masands never troubled Punjab Kaur.

A few weeks after this incident, when the Guru was at Paunta, his second wife Sundri gave birth to prince Ajit Singh. Great rejoicings took place. Salutes were fired from the fortresses of Nahan and Srinagar. The ladies gave alms to the poor and gifts to dependents. Disciples from distant places came and presented beautiful clothes and ornaments to the prince.

# CHAPTER XIII.

As has been said in a previous chapter, the daughter of Fateh Shah of Srinagar was betrothed to Ajmere Chand, son of Raja Bhim Chand of Bilaspur. Guru Govind Singh was invited to participate in the marriage festivities at Srinagar and was asked to take with him all of his attendants. The Guru did not avail himself of the invitation as he was afraid lest the splendour of his retinue might rekindle the fire of jealousy in the breast of Bhim Chand. But to show that he valued the friendship of Fateh Shah he sent Diwan Nand Chand and Prohit Daya Ram with a hundred *Sowars* to present *tambol.* It consisted of gifts valued at a lac and a quarter of rupees. The marriage came off with great *eclat.*

When the time of receiving *tambol* came the presents of the Guru were announced amongst others. No kinsman of Fateh Shah, from among the Rajas present, had given him *tambol* of such value. This out-bidding annoyed them all. Bhim Chand was particularly furious. Raja Kirpal Chand Katochia and Raja Bir Sen of Mandi, at heart inimical to Bhim Chand, excited him still more. He sent for Fateh Shah and threatened him with the severance of the newly contracted tie in case he continued to keep any friendly intercourse with the Guru. At first Fateh Shah protested against Bhim Chand's behaviour towards the Guru; but when the infuriated Chief of Bilaspur actually carried out his threat and departed from Srinagar with his son, leaving the bride behind, he gave way. It was, then, agreed upon that the *tambol* sent by the Guru be plundered and not a man be left alive to take the tidings to the Guru. Noticing the change in Fateh Shah's demenour and divining his motive, Diwan Nand Chand and his attendants forthwith drew their swords and fought their way to Paunta. A report was made to the Guru that Bhim Chand and his confederate Rajas were coming up on Paunta. Immediately ammunition was distributed to the men and the fortress was placed in a state of defence.

When a handful of the Guru's men escaped unhurt, Bhim Chand collected all the confederate Rajas and in an excited speech appealed to them to help him in either killing the Guru or sending him in custody to Aurangzebe who would deal with him as he had done with his father, Guru Tegh Bahadur. The appeal was listened to. Rajas Bhim Chand, Fateh Shah, Kirpal Chand of Kangra, Bir Sen of Mandi, Kesri Singh of Jaswal, Hari Chand of Handur, Dyal Chand of Kot Garh and about twenty others put their respective armies in motion amidst the beat of drums and the shouts of the populace. On the side of the Guru Mohri Chand, Gulab Rai, Sahib Chand, Hari Chand, Kirpal Chand, Prohit Daya Ram, Jaita, Rana Sanga, Jowahirji, Udaji and other veterans advanced to meet the Rajas. Bribed by the Rajas the Pathans who had been employed on the recommendation of Budhu Shah went over to the enemy a few hours before the battle. Only Kale Khan and his hundred men remained loyal. Five or six hundred Udasi Sadhus who had been daily feeding themselves on the Guru's bounty, fearing lest they too might be called upon to engage in the fight, took advantage of the darkness of the night and fled. Only Sadhu Kirpal Das refused to accompany the fugitives and remained behind to live or die with the Guru.

# CHAPTER XIV.

The Rajas and their advisers had supposed that when the Pathans were alienated from the Guru he would have no fighting men left; but as it was subsequently proved, in this belief they were mistaken. The low-caste, unwarlike men who had been hitherto looked upon with contempt and who had never been heard of in the history of Indian warfare proved more than a match for the Rajputs and Pathans combined. The Guru had perfect faith in his men. Leaving Ram Kaur, Mehra, and Kala in charge of the Paunta fortress and accompanied by his uncle Kirpal Chand, Sahib Chand, Lal Chand, son of Bidhi Chand, whose wondrous feats of valour in the time of Guru Har Govind have won him a name in Sikh history, Diwan Nand Chand, Lal Chand, confectioner, Udai Singh, Bachittar Singh, Alam Singh and Chandan Rai the Guru marched out at the head of a few hundred devoted followers to give battle to the enemy.

Arriving at the maidan of Bhangani, a village some 8 miles from Paunta, he observed the armies of the Rajas and the detachment of Pathans coming down in full speed. A halt was immediately ordered. Commandant Sango Shah advanced with half of the Guru's detachment, the other half being kept in reserve. The hill armies, thereupon, fired volleys of bullets and the battle ensued. Sango Shah stationed his men in a ravine which served as a rampart. A strong wind blowing in the face of the hill army increased the swiftness of the arrows shot by the Sikhs and created an impression that even the elements were partial to the Guru. When Rajas Hari Chand, Bhim Chand and Fateh Shah came near enough the Sikh bullets killed about a thousand men and repulsed the enemy. Kesri Singh, brother-in-law of Bhim Chand, seeing this came to their help. The disloyal Pathans tempted by the hope of plunder eagerly came forward. But the bullets and arrows of the Sikhs impeded their progress. Reinforced by five hundred horsemen, led by Prohit Daya Ram and Diwan Nand Chand, the Sikhs pierced the breasts of the hillmen by their arrows and laid hundreds of them prostrate. Just when the battle was raging furiously, Budhu Shah, with four sons, two brothers and a thousand followers, arrived to atone for the treachery of the Pathans who had been employed on his recommendation, and fell upon a section of the Rajput army. This fidelity and sacrifice delighted the Guru. Kale Khan, with his hundred men, was sent in aid of Budhu Shah. The battle, thus raged in three places, divided the strength of the enemy. At this time Lal Chand Mahi, the Guru's wrestler, feeling a strong impulse ran his horse into the thick of the fight where Sango Shah and his brothers were fighting the enemy, and although he was unpractised in the art of war his poniard killed so many that when at last he fell the air resounded with shouts of bravo !, bravo !, bravo !, from all sides. His example was imitated by Lal Chand, confectioner, who had never handled a weapon. Bowing to the Guru with a sword and a shield in his hands he joined

Prohit Daya Ram and Diwan Nand Chand and spreading havoc in the ranks of the Afghan traitors died bravely. Mohri Chand next rushed into the ranks of the Pathans and struck down many; but surrounded by the foe he was seriously wounded. Chandan Rai and Sango Ram, with fifty men, came to Mohri's help and after rescuing him fought bravely on the side of Commandant Sango Shah. Meanwhile Budhu Shah was performing great deeds of valour and although his two sons and many followers had fallen in the battle, he was inflicting heavy losses on the enemy. Soon after he was reinforced by the Guru's uncle, Kirpal Chand, from whose arrows death rained on the invading army. A detachment of the enemy then directed their arrows to the spot from where Guru Govind Singh was watching the progress of the fight; but it was repulsed by the fury of the missiles thrown from there. At this stage taunted by Bhim Chand and other Rajput Rajas, Hayat Khan and other Pathans fell upon the main line of the Sikhs. The air resounded with the cries of Ali! Ali! Ali! The Rajput forces also joined in the fight. Arrows and bullets poured down in torrents. Men and horses fell in large numbers. Several Rajput princes were slain. Observing the Pathans advancing from a flank, Udasi Kirpal Das, taking hold of a mace, struck it forcibly on Hayat Khan's head. The man's skull was broken and brains scattered. His friend Najabat Khan was about to cut the Sadhu into pieces when Diwan Nand Chand struck the Pathan with a spear.

The wound inflicted was, however, slight. Recovering from the shock Najabat Khan together with Bhikhan Khan fell upon Diwan Nand Chand. But the Guru's uncle Kirpal Chand, Lal Chand, Sahib Chand, Ganga Ram and Daya Ram Prohit engaged with the Pathans and were about to put them to flight when Raja Ghazi Chand of Chanderi attacked the Sikhs from behind; and so ably did he fight that the Sikhs would have been compelled to retire had not Udai Singh, Bachittar Singh, and other Rajput refugees come to their help and turned the tide of war. And though Rajas Hari Chand and Gopal Chand, aided by Raja Kesri Singh, fought bravely the confederate army fell back. The heroic Ghazi Chand, true to the name he bore and Najabat Khan, unable to bear the ignominy of defeat, fell upon the Sikh Commandant Sango Shah. The latter was killed in a hand to hand fight with Najabat Khan.

The loss of Sango Shah and Mohri instead of disheartening the Sikhs only served to inspire them with the courage born of despair. Death rained from their arrows. Numerous Pathans fell dead. Bhikhan Khan received a wound and fled. His flight created confusion in the ranks of the hill-men. The veteran Hari Chand, recovering from his wounds, again appeared on the scene, killed Jit Mal and inflicted several wounds on Guru Govind Singh. But his death approached. The Guru's arrow felled him down. His kinsman Raja Fateh Shah fought like a lion to wreak vengeance on the Sikhs and victory would have been theirs; but the arrival of two wooden batteries that had been prepared by a Sikh carpenter, Rama, strengthened the hands of the Sikhs. Shells of stone rained upon the mountaineers and crushed them to death. Panic-struck the enemy fled in all directions. The victorious Sikhs put the flying Pathans and hill-men to the sword, plundered stores of ammunition and provisions and returned to their quarters singing the glory of the Lord of Hosts who had granted them victory. On their arrival at Paunta great rejoicings took place to celebrate the victory.

# CHAPTER XV.

This was the first battle the Guru had fought and the first victory he had won. Several of his brave friends and near kinsmen had fallen in the battle; but this dispirited him not. Budhu Shah who had lost two sons, a brother, and hundreds of followers, and Sant Kirpal Das who had fought so well, were rewarded with a grant of the Guru's turbans which were tokens of undying friendship.

Some weeks after the battle of Bhangani the Guru left Paunta. Raja Maidni Parkash who had throughout remained loyal to the Guru, presented him with valuable parting gifts. For a week he halted at Loh Garh from where the great Baba Banda fought against the Imperial army for years. Thus stopping at various places and spreading the light of Faith, a detailed account of which cannnot be given in this short narrative, he arrived at Anandpur where he was accorded a hearty welcome.

During the three years' absence of the Guru from Anandpur, Aurangzebe's bigotry, obstinately continued in defiance of the solemn warnings he had received in other parts of the Empire, provoked serious discontent in the Punjab. As Guru Govind Singh was the spiritual Lord of the Hindus and Sikhs who regarded him as Sacha Padshah (real King) nay as an emblem of the Divine Being Himself, it was only natural that people should have flocked to him with their complaints. Their tales of woe and wrong, the heartless indifference of the profligate Muslim officials to the troubles of the Hindus, the reduction of respectable Hindus into slavery, the forcible removal of Hindu virgins into the seraglios of the Muslim gentry and nobility pained him deeply. He was convinced that the oppressors had exhausted human tolerance and that time had come for the adoption of some plan of retribution. So he employed all the force of his eloquence in telling the people that they should no longer meekly submit to Muslim tyranny, that they should return blow for blow and should not rest till they wreaked vengeance on their oppressors. The influence of this teaching permeated the whole of North Western India. In other parts of the country too, the information of the new movement inspired the Hindus with courage in their struggle for freedom.

With a view to prepare for future contingencies the Guru now started a factory at Anandpur for the manufacture of guns, swords, ammunition and other implements of war. Henceforth though the disciples from the war-like tribes of the North-West continued to supply weapons of the best steel and finest make, the Guru was no longer dependent for war materials on this source alone.

At this time mother Nanaki who had played no small part in moulding the character of her illustrious son, Guru Teg Bahadur, and still more illustrious grandson, Guru Govind Singh, passed away, after living long enough to see her great-grandson, prince Ajit Singh, the boy martyr, who subsequently fought so bravely at the siege of Chamkour.

After the battle of Bhangani, the hill Rajas, convinced that it was no easy matter to crush the Guru, thought it prudent to court his favour. Their leader, Bhim Chand, accompanied by his Minister, Parma Nand, came to the Guru to ask for forgiveness for his past conduct. The Guru accused him of having waged a war which had resulted in the death of so many brave men on both sides; but as no good could be expected from the prolongation of the quarrel he forgave the Raja and his allies.

In the year 1688-89 A. D. four fortresses, Anand Garh, Loh Garh, Fateh Garh and Kes Garh were built in the vicinity of Anandpur. Of these Anandgarh proved most serviceable during the siege of Anandpur by the Imperial army.

To test the fidelity and patience of the Sikhs the Guru once ordered that no Sikh should leave Anandpur without his permission. Guards were stationed at all gates to prevent egress. Many of those who were loud in their professions of love for the Guru were the first to grow impatient for seeing the world outside. Before a week passed they adopted curious plans for getting out. One device was particularly very ingenious. A person was made to feign death. He was placed on a bier and taken to the cremation ground accompanied by a regular crowd who all the while kept on singing funeral songs. When the procession passed out of the town, the Guru who had somehow divined the secret ordered the party to halt. The body was placed on a funeral pyre and when preparations were being made to cremate it the man who had hitherto lain motionless threw off funeral attire and fled to the jungle to the confusion of the men who had resorted to this fraudulent practice and to the astonishment and laughter of the beholders. The incident greatly embarassed the delinquents and confirmed the impression that the Guru was a knower of hearts and that it was impossible to deceive him.

# CHAPTER XVI.

Aurangzebe was at this time engaged in quelling disturbances in the Deccan. Reinforcements were sent from the Punjab. The military strength of the Province was considerably reduced. The revenue fell in to arrears. No one cared to collect tribute from the hill Rajas. When a few crores of rupees were demanded for the Imperial treasury, the Governor of the Punjab expressed his inability to comply. This excited the wrath of the Emperor. Commandant Miyan Khan was sent to apply force and obtain the money. On arrival at Lahore he marched against the Rajas, west of Ravi, and sent his nephew Alif Khan against Raja Kirpal Chand of Kangra and the Rajas of the adjoining hills. Kirpal Chand and Dyal Chand paid the tribute. They suggested to Alif Khan that the realization of the tribute from all the hill Rajas would be a comparatively easy task if their chief, Bhim Chand, was taught to respect the power of the Imperial arms. The suggestion was adopted and a punitive force marched against Bilaspur. A halt was ordered in the plain of Nadaon from where a messenger was sent to Bhim Chand to tell him that in case he did not pay three years' tribute immediately he would be taken prisoner and his territory looted. The threat failed in its effect. The Raja flew into rage on learning that it was at the instigation of his enemy Kirpal Chand that the expedition was coming against him. A council of war was held in all haste and it was unanimously resolved that the advancing Moghals should be opposed.

The allied Rajas brought their respective forces and a battle commenced. The Rajputs fought well; but they could not hope to continue the struggle against so powerful an enemy. So when the night fell and the Rajas met at dinner they resolved to seek the Guru's aid; and with this view they forthwith despatched an embassy to Anandpur. At first Guru Govind Singh hesitated to enter into an alliance with so treacherous a people; but when Wazir Parma Nand, Prime Minister of the Raja of Bilaspur, fell at his feet and when he considered that the time was not distant when he himself would have to offer resistance to this very same power he decided to proffer assistance. Diwan Nand Chand was ordered to take five hundred chosen men and before it was dawn the Guru himself reached Nadaon with a considerable force. The arrival of the Sikhs strengthened the failing hearts of the hill men. At noon the battle was recommenced. The arrows of the Sikhs wrought havoc in the ranks of the Mussalman army. Raja Dyal Chand, Alif Khan's ally, was killed by an arrow, shot by the Guru, and when his friend Kirpal Chand, too, was wounded the Muslim Army lost heart and retreated under cover of darkness. Bhim Chand and the confederate Rajas expressed their gratitude to the Guru and pressed him to stay with them and enjoy their hospitality; but very soon after it transpired that Bhim Chand had made a private treaty with Alif Khan by virtue of which he was allowed to pay tribute in small instalments on condition that he should keep aloof and let Alif Khan realize the tribute from the confederate Rajas in such manner as might appear proper to him. The intelligence spread alarm in the Rajput circles. The Guru took offence at this and left Bilaspur in sheer disgust. And though Bhim Chand endeavoured to conciliate him by the offer of costly presents to the Sikh soldiery he bluntly told the treacherous hill chieftain that he could put no faith in men who worshipped stocks and stones and whose hearts were dead as stones.

The passage of the Sikh soldiery, on their way to Anandpur, was opposed by the Rajputs of the village of Alsoon who were the clansmen of Bhim Chand. On previous occasions, too, these men had murdered and plundered the Sikh pilgrims. So the Sikhs fell upon the villagers. With the exception of old men, women and children, all who opposed their advance were put to the sword. In this way inflicting condign punishment on these high-way robbers the Sikhs marched forward. The treatment of the Alsoon Rajputs inspired the whole hill population with a feeling of awe for the Sikhs. No further difficulty was, therefore, encountered till their return to Anandpur.

The Guru's wife Jeetoji had no offspring till now. She had, times out of number, prayed to the Guru for being blessed with a son; but had as often met with the reply that such a gift was not in his power to grant. Now Jeetoji had constantly seen people coming to the Guru and receiving blessings which had invariably resulted in the satiation of their desires. She was at a loss to understand her husband's refusal to her repeated prayers. At length she took courage and asked for an explanation. The Guru enquired from her if she remembered what he invariably told all who came to him with some request or other. "Serve the poor and the needy and the *Sadh Sangat* (assemblies of pious persons)" was the reply. "Do thou likewise," said the Guru, "and the Timeless One will grant thy prayer." The command was respectfully obeyed. The wife of the Sachcha Padshah, whom the mightiest of the mighty worshipped and adored, was daily seen washing the feet of the pilgrims to Adandpur and serving in the cooking and the dining rooms. The Sikhs naturally disliked such offices from such an august lady but none dared object. The services had the effect desired. The Sikh devotees filled with emotion fervently wished her Heaven's chociest blessings. Their prayer was heard and the illustrious lady was blessed with a son on the 21st of Chet, *Samvat* Vikrimadittya 1747, according to 1640 A. D., who was named Jhujhar Singh and who received martydom in the battle of Chamkour.

The assistance that the Guru had rendered to Raja Bhim Chand of Bilaspur and the other confederate Rajas and which had contributed to the defeat of Alif Khan, was, of course, calculated to offend Dilawar Khan, Subah of Lahore. Not many months had elapsed before a campaign was organised and sent against the Guru, under the leadership of the Subah's son, Rustam Khan. The invading army encamped in the bed of a hill torrent near Anandpur at nightfall. The Guru, timely informed, immediately ordered an advance against the foe. The night was dark. The air resounded with the war cries of the

Sikhs and the noise of the arrows, as they flew into the ranks of the enemy, created an exaggerated impression regarding the number of the Sikh assailants. Even the elements seemed to side with the Sikhs. The rain fell in torrents and the waters of the hill stream swept off great many Mussalmans and compelled the rest to flee for their lives.

Thus discomfited the enemy returned to Lahore to the great chagrin of the Subah whose rage knew no bounds and who now burned with a desire to wreak vengeance on the man who was the author of so much disgrace to him. His adopted son, Husaini, a fierce and unrelentful person, was now placed in command of another expedition against the Guru, with Alif Khan, Kripa Ram, and Chandan Singh, Raja of Nurpur, as his Lieutenants. On his way Husaini first plundered Amarkot, subdued the Dhadwals and ravaged the Dun. He put to the sword many other hill chieftains of note and devastated their territories. The report of his cruel deeds spread far and wide. Bhim Chand of Bilaspur and his ally Kirpal Chand Katochia, forgetting that it was the Guru's support of them that had led the Governor of Lahore to wage war on him, joined Husaini and offered their services for the subjugation of Anandpur and the capture of its Lord. The report of this treacherous conduct was brought to the Guru who gave orders that Anandpur be placed in a state of defence. Diwan Nand Chand was placed in command of the garrison. The intelligence of the expected attack filled the minds of many an easy-going

Sikh with terror. Unused to the hardships of war and accustomed to a life of ease they saw in these Muslim invasions the approaching collapse of the time-honoured structure that the Gurus had raised. They waited upon the Guru's mother and asked her to persuade her son to make peace with Husaini on any terms. But the device failed. The Guru refused to listen to such an humiliating proposal. He had been commissioned, said he, to put an end to the atrocities of the ruling race. To submit to their authority was, therefore, out of question.

Meantime Husaini was marching on Anandpur. Raja Gopal Chand of Goler, afraid of the cruelties of the barbarous invader, met him on the way and offered a part of the tribute. But Kirpal Chand and Bhim Chand advised Husaini to arrest Gopal Chand and demand the whole amount due. Gopal Chand contrived to escape and shut himself up in the fortress of Goler together with his ally Raja Ram Singh. Husaini laid siege to Goler. Hard pressed by the scarcity of provisions, and of both men and ammunition, the Raja of Goler sent his Wazir to Husaini suing for peace. Husaini demanded ten thousand rupees. Sangtia Singh, with half a dozen other Sirdars and a few hundred men, was sent to bring the Raja. Solemn promises were given that the Raja would not be molested. Gopal Chand came; but no agreement could be arrived at. Kirpal Chand Katochia, bidding adieu to his solemn obligations, suggested his capture or assassination. The effort failed. Gopal came to know of the sinister design and escaped to his camp.

The battle now raged furiously. On both sides there was a great loss of life. Bhim Chand's ally, Kirpal Chand, and Sangtia Singh, both fell, but the loss of the Muslims was great. Bhim Chand sought safety in flight and Husaini, who had boasted that he would take the Guru prisoner to Lahore, was killed. Gopal won the battle. Thus ended the second Muslim attempt to invade Anandpur.

Dilawar Khan again sent Shaur Khan against the Guru with a large army; but his passage was opposed by the Raja of Jaswal in whose territory a decisive battle was fought. Jhujhar Singh and Narain Chand, Rajput warriors, who commanded Muslim forces, fell fighting bravely. Their death dispirited the Muslim force which, under the pretext of sickness, returned to Lahore.

Enraged at so many reverses to the Muslim arms Aurangzebe placed his eldest son, Muazzam, in command of a large imperial force in the year 1701 A. D. The Prince himself proceeded to Lahore and sent his Lieutenants to collect the tribute and punish the Rajas who refused to make immediate payment of all the arrears. They met with success everywhere. The Moghul officer who visited Anandpur noticed with admiration the bounteous manner in which the poor and the needy were fed and looked after. So favourably impressed was he with all that he saw that he took upon himself the duty of punishing the hill chieftains who had hitherto given some trouble or other to the Sikh Colony at Anandpur. The faces of great many were blackened and placed on donkeys they were carried from village to village amidst the cries and taunts of the street imps. Very few of them escaped ignominous treatment at the hands of the Moghuls.

This exceptional attention to the Guru roused an angry feeling in the breasts of the hill Rajas. Much time had not elapsed before they formed a deputation under the leadership of Ajmer Chand, son of Bhim Chand of Bilaspur, and waited upon the Governor of Lahore with a complaint that Guru Gobind Singh had stored large quantities of ammunition. Thousands of brave outlaws were in his employ. He had command of a large treasury to which all his disciples contributed one-tenth of their income. His whole energies and resources were devoted to converting the Sikhs into a militant power. This was why there was so much unrest in all parts of the country where the Sikhs lived. If this danger was not nipped in the bud they were afraid the time was not distant when the Sikhs would be emboldened to measure swords with the Imperial Government. The Subah of Lahore was already prejudiced against the Guru. To convert him to this belief was not a difficult task. So on the old charge of his aiding the hill Rajas in the battles of Nadaon and Goler he sent a considerable force against the Guru with orders that a fine of Rs. 10,000 be realized from him and in case he refused compliance he should be captured and brought to Lahore as a prisoner. In pursuance of this order the Subah's son, accompanied by the Naib Nazim, Dalel Khan, attacked Anandpur in the following spring and, although the Sikhs bravely resisted, the invaders entered the town, massacred a large number of people and taking away all they could lay their hands upon they halted at the village Bhalon, some 8 miles from Anandpur. Flushed with victory they drank, sang and danced till late in the night. When they thus lay drunk the Sikhs fell upon them. This tiger-like bounce spread panic in the whole Muslim camp. What for the darkness of the night and what for the consternation caused by this sudden attack there was great confusion in the Muslim invading force. In darkness and uproar friends struck friends. A great many fled for their lives and of the splendid force that had fought so bravely a few hours previous not a soul remained. The Sikhs captured large stores and ammunition which more than counterbalanced the property the Muslims had plundered.

Another expedition was being organised against the Guru when through the influence of Bhai Nand Lal and Diwan Hakim Rai of Agra who were the Guru's disciples prince Muazzam forbade further operations against him. The prince had ambitions of his own. Though he was the eldest son of Aurangzebe, and thus rightful heir to the Mughul throne, he knew that when his old sire died he would have to fight for what was his by right, according to the traditional practice in his family. It was, therefore, his interest to secure as many supporters as he could get. With this view he sent Diwan Nand Lal to Anandpur praying for the Guru's aid, both spiritual and temporal. The prayer was granted. The Guru assured Diwan Nand Lal that by God's grace Muazzam would be made Emperor of Delhi. The prince was greatly pleased at the success that had attended Diwan Nand Lal's mission and rewarded him with befitting honours.

Now that through the intervention of prince Muazzam peace reigned in the northern Punjab the Guru's whole time was taken up with the propagation of spiritual and secular knowledge. The Pundits and poets in his employ illumined the minds of the disciples from distant lands who came to receive the solace of religion. Those times were, however, of anarchy and confusion. The pilgrims to Anandpur were not unoften molested by both Hindus and Muhammadans. Their numbers instead of affording them security tempted evil-disposed persons who, under the impression that the Sikhs carried valuables on their persons, committed raids upon them, taking away what they could and causing no small loss of life. It is noteworthy to remark that notwithstanding these troubles the Sikh pilgrims continued to visit Anandpur in large numbers to pay their homage to the Guru. At length the state of things became unbearable and when the Ranghars of Bajrur, a clan of fierce Mussalmans, made it a regular profession to molest the Sikh pilgrims a Sikh force surrounded their village. The Ranghars fought for a while; but at length gave way and fled. The village was looted and much of the plundered property of the Sikh pilgrims was restored to their owners.

# CHAPTER XVII.

The conservative population of the hills never forgave the Sikhs for their novel ways and beliefs and gave them no end of annoyance. The lands attached to Anandpur did not yield sufficient produce for the ever-growing Sikh colony. The Sikhs were consequently compelled to go to the Jungles and to the villages adjoining to procure grass and fuel and purchase provisions. The people of these villages generally gave trouble on these occasions. The Sikhs were, therefore, not infrequently compelled to employ force in providing themselves with the necessaries of life. The result was constant conflicts between the Sikhs and the hill men. The hill potentates took sides with their clansmen and instead of exercising their influence in favour of peace and facilitating the purchase of supplies they invariably resorted to menaces and threats which made matters still worse. The hatred of the Sikhs also for the hill Rajputs knew no bounds. Leaving apart the many petty acts of persecution on the part of the hill men their princes had many a time borrowed strength from Mussalmans to exterminate the Sikhs. It was when the feeling between the two peoples was very high that the Guru, while on an hunting expedition, with a party of his followers, was waylaid by Raja Bhim Chand who was lying in ambush with a considerable force. The Sikhs, though taken by surprise, repulsed the attack and inflicted heavy losses on the assailants. The other Rajas, hearing of this, held a council at which it was decided to turn out the Guru from Anandpur with the help of the Moghal Emperor. A man was immediately sent to Sirhind with the message that Guru Govind Singh had organised a military caste with a view to wreak vengeance on the Moghuls. This people had spread anarchy and confusion in the territories of the Rajas. Life and property were not safe. All provisions were being plundered and land laid waste.

Aurangzebe was, at this time, engaged in wars in the Deccan. On the receipt of the message he sent orders for the suppression of the rising Sikh power. Adina Beg, Moghal Commander, with Painda Khan, a brave Pathan, as his Lieutenant, started against the Guru with 10,000 men. The Rajas also brought their men to help the Moghul Commander. On the approach of the allied army the war drum was beaten. The Sikhs immediately prepared themselves for fight. A battle was fought at which Painda Khan fell in an hand to hand fight with the Guru. Prince Ajit Singh, attended by veteran warriors, committed tremendous slaughter in the ranks of the hill men and routed them completely. Adina Beg finding himself at a disadvantage thought it prudent to retreat and returned to Sirhind.

This reverse did not dispirit the Rajas. They again met at Bilaspur and resolved to make another effort to subjugate the Sikhs. On this occasion they were helped by a renowned warrior Azmatullah, leader of the Gujjars, residing in those parts. The Guru's army was strengthened by reinforcements from Manjha, Malwa and the North-West Punjab. The fortresses of Fateh Garh, Loh Garh and Anand Garh were garrisoned. The command of Manjha Sikhs was entrusted to Daya Singh and that of the Malwa Sikhs to Prince Ajit Singh. The hill army surrounded the Sikhs, on all sides, and though they fought with their usual gallantry the brave Azmatulla and his men compelled them to abandon many a position of vantage. Noticing this Prince Ajit Singh and the veterans Udai Singh, Bachittar Singh, Subegh Singh and others displayed so great skill and valour that the Sikhs were, at length, able to hold their ground. Azmatulla was surrounded by a flank movement and killed by a sword thrust. The hill men were naturally disheartened; but the fight continued till sunset, when both armies retired to their camps.

During the night the Rajas held a council and resolved upon blockading Anandpur with a view to starve the Sikhs and thus force them to submit. The Guru somehow got scent of this and when early at dawn the Rajputs surrounded Anandpur and set about pitching their tents, the arrows and bullets of the Sikhs forced them to retreat. Prince Ajit Singh then called on his men to fall upon the retreating Rajputs and slew large numbers of them. The glad tidings was soon conveyed to the Guru who blessed his promising son and his officers who had maintained the dignity of the Sikh name. At night when the Rajas again met at supper Kesri Singh Jaswalia with a view to raise the spirits of his colleagues offered to lead his mad elephant against the Guru and bring him a prisoner. At this time the Rajas were in a frame of mind in which anything that could give a ray of hope was of immense relief. Kesri Singh was a braggart. His intention was no sooner expressed than it was known throughout the Sikh camp. The Guru desired Duni Chand, leader of the Manjha contingent, to face the elephant and put him to death; but the man fled at the dead of night and died of snake-bite on his way home. Next morning Kesri Singh, with the mad elephant in front of him, advanced with his army against the Guru. When the elephant came near enough Bachittar Singh Rajput rode towards him, thrust his spear into the animal's mailed forehead and pierced it through. The wounded brute, then, shot back into the Rajput ranks and trampled hundreds under his feet. Raja Kesri Singh pranced his feet restlessly, right and left, when Udai Singh fell upon him and throwing him off his horse cut off his head and lifting it on one end of his spear brought it triumphantly to his camp.

The death of such a valiant comrade instead of disheartening the hill Rajas increased their rage. So during the battle of the day following they fought so bravely that the Sikhs had to twice retreat to their fortresses. The blockading force was, however, not sufficiently strong to turn out the Sikhs from their sheltering places. For weeks the battle raged; but no prospect of the Sikhs giving way was visible. At length on the suggestion of Pamma, a priest at the court of the Raja of Kahloor, whose hated name has been handed down to posterity, the Rajas had recourse to a stratagem. A cow was stationed near the principal gate of the town. In a billet placed on its neck the Guru was told that the Rajas had made a mistake in waging war against him. They would have returned to their homes long ago; but they were afraid lest this act of theirs might be interpreted as cowardice on their part. They were the Guru's cows and as such besought him to protect their honour. If he vacated Anandpur for a day they would raise the blockade and retire. After the lapse of this period he might reoccupy the town. The stratagem was successful. The Guru granted the appeal. The Sikhs on vacating Anandpur encamped at Nirmogarh, a couple of miles off. As was expected instead of retiring from the field the hill Rajas fell upon the Sikhs and the latter were exposed on all sides. Victory, however, declared itself for them. A cannon ball, directed against the Guru, reduced his attendant Ram Singh to atoms; but the Guru himself was not hurt. His missiles, on the contrary, slew a large number of the assailants. At length, finding that even in the open the Sikhs were invincible, the invading army retreated. Meantime, in response to an appeal, made by the Rajas, Wazir Khan, Governor of Sirhind, brought reinforcements. Thus strengthened the hill men again invested the Sikhs. But the onslaughts of the latter, under Prince Ajit Singh, made it difficult for the allied armies to turn them out from their positions. The Sikh chroniclers say that Wazir Khan, finding that the Sikhs were a formidable foe to deal with, proposed to the Guru through the Raja of Basali that in case he retired to the latter's dominions the siege would be raised and that pressed by his advisers the Guru complied with the request. The truth, however, seems to be that when, some days after, the Sikhs suffered a reverse the Guru retreated to Basali, in the dominion of a friendly Raja in the neighbourhood of Anandpur and sheltered himself in the fortress there, and that the invading army did not consider it worth while to follow him. Here he stopped for some time, and resumed his occupations of peace.

# CHAPTER XVIII.

Raja Dharmpal of Basali became a sincere admirer of the Guru. He exhausted all his resources to do him honour and remained in constant attendance on him. The time, at length, arrived, when the Guru had to leave Basali, with a view to re-occupy Anandpur. He acknowledged the Raja's attentions and blessed him with a promise of undying friendship. On the way, a halt was ordered at Bhambaur with whose chief the Guru had become acquainted while at Basali. He passed some months at this place and employed his time in spreading his doctrines. The disciples on hearing of his long sojourn here came from places, far and near, and brought him offerings. A party of them was way-laid and plundered by the ruffians of a village called Kalmot. When the information reached the Guru he ordered a band of Sikh sepoys to punish the offending villagers and recover the plundered property. This was forthwith done and from that time forward the Sikhs were not molested by that people. Not long after the Guru returned to Anandpur and repopulated it. The retreating hill Rajas and Mussalmans had not forgotten to destroy its fortifications and pull down its important edifices.

A young disciple Jog Singh was very assiduous in the service of the Guru who naturally favoured him most. This excited jealousy and when, one day, he went abroad alone he was way-laid and assaulted. He bore the treatment with forbearance and did not mention the incident to any one. When the Guru, somehow, heard of the matter he sent for Jog Singh and asked him why he had failed to report the affair to him. Jog Singh replied that nothing extraordinary had occurred that necessitated a report to the Guru. The Guru alone was the subject of his thoughts and the kisses or kicks of people did not engross his mind. This exhibition of self-abnegation highly pleased the Guru and the followers in whose hearing the statement had been made. It is ardent admirers, all confiding and all sacrificing, such as Jog Singh, that followed the Guru's banner in his efforts to release the people from spiritual and political slavery.

At this time the hill Rajas were at peace with the Guru. Experience had taught them to respect the Guru's authority. Their ambassadors, at the Guru's Court, chiefly Pamma, whose name has become an opprobrious epithet in Sikh terminology, employed their diplomacy and smooth tongues in keeping the Sikhs in humour. During these days of amity and accord the Guru was persuaded to visit Rawalsar, a sacred lake, in the vicinity of Suket. On the day of 'Ikadasi' when most of the hill Rajas were assembled, at that seat of pilgrimage, the Guru again addressed them on their abject condition, and the means for their amelioration, and so effective was his speech that a great many of them volunteered to receive the Sikh baptism; but unluckily their Brahman advisers dissuaded them from taking the step and thus prevented the formation of a coalition which would have considerably facilitated the work of India's regeneration. Thus the great scheme which the illustrious Sikh leader had formulated was opposed, from its very start, by a large and influential section of the very people in whose interests it had been conceived and adopted. And, as will be shown, in the following pages, these very hill Rajas were instrumental in the ultimate defeat of the Guru and the scattering of the Sikh forces when the Imperial troops advanced against the Guru and almost annihilated his political influence, during the last siege of Anandpur.

The splendour of the Guru's court, at this time, surpassed even that of the Moghul Emperors. All that could add to its brilliancy and enhance its glory was there. The Moghul Emperor had a throne of gold at Delhi. The Sikhs would not rest contented unless a temple of gold was erected at the seat of their Guru's government. Accordingly fabulous quantities of gold poured in from all parts of the country. The edifice was erected in a surprisingly short time and the Sikh Scriptures were installed therein.

Riches and worldly splendour have always exercised a vitiating influence on public morals. The wide-awake Guru saw that the accumulation of riches on which subsisted the large body of his retainers was proving hurtful to them. Men were becoming greedy and were losing reverence for the higher ideals of life. To eradicate the evil and show his supreme contempt for riches all costly raiments were put to the flame and the treasure thrown into the Sutlej. Thenceforward it was ruled that the Guru and all his dependents should live in the strictest simplicity. This act of the Guru elicited adverse comment. Most of the parasites that had fed upon public alms gave out that the intellect of the Guru had become demented and that he was making it impossible for his followers to strengthen his hands. The great majority of the followers had, however, implicit faith in the Guru's judgment and unmurmuringly obeyed him in all things. They still remember how abstemiously the Guru passed the latter part of his life and none of his principles has taken a deeper root in the Sikh mind than the belief that it is a sin to live luxuriantly upon public offerings.

Not unlike his illustrious predecessor, Baba Nanak, the Guru took pleasure in visiting principal places of pilgrimage and eradicating superstitious beliefs. In 1702 A. D., accompanied by his mother and family and attended by a strong body-guard, the Guru left Anandpur to attend an Eclipse Fair at Thaneswar. Arriving there he preached the pure doctrines of his creed and to show that he had no faith in the absurd notions, prevalent at the time, such as the belief that the offering of a cow facilitated the journey of a pilgrim, after death, the Guru offered an ass instead. The novelty excited general attention and when an explanation was asked the Guru thoroughly exposed such superstitions and asked the people to look to God alone for protection, whether in this world or the next.

The visit of the Guru to Thaneswar gave an occasion to the hill Rajas to again start conspiracies against him. It was known that the Guru's escort consisted of a few hundred men alone. So with a force of a few thousand men it was thought that it would not be a difficult task to intercept him, on his way back to Anandpur, and put him easily to death. Said Beg and Alif Khan, Muslim commanders, were marching towards Lahore, with a large force. The hill Rajas, aided by the Pathans of Ropar, persuaded the Generals to wait for the arrival of the Guru and annihilate him and his small party. When the Guru encamped in the vicinity of Chamkour the Moghuls fell upon him. The Sikhs fought with such desperate valour that Said Beg Khan, moved by a feeling of admiration, came over to the Guru and prayed for permission to serve the Sikh cause. The desertion of Said Beg dispirited Alif Khan and compelled him to order a retreat. Thus ended a cowardly attempt to take the life of one who was so unselfishly working in behalf of the very men who were conspiring for his life.

# CHAPTER XIX.

Immediately after the battle described in the last chapter the Guru returned to Anandpur and resumed his usual avocations. One day a Brahman came to him with a complaint that when he was returning home, with his newly married wife, Jabbar Khan, a leading Pathan of Bassi, forcibly took her to his house and detained her there. He had, in vain, endeavoured to appeal for help to all men of influence in the locality. He was confident that the Guru, who was a protector of the poor, would rescue his bride and restore her to him. The appeal to the Guru was successful. Prince Ajit Singh was immediately ordered to rescue the woman and bring her ravisher, bound hand and foot, to Anandpur. Early at dawn, when the people were still asleep, prince Ajit Singh and his party forced their entrance into the village. Those who opposed were put to the sword. Jabbar Khan was captured and brought to Anandpur. The Brahman's wife was restored to him. Jabbar Khan was put to death and so exemplary was the punishment accorded that for years following the crime was not repeated.

The Sikhs never forgave the treacherous conduct of the hill men in waylaying the Guru when he was returning from Thaneswar with a small escort. Whenever they found an opportunity they wreaked their vengeance on the perpetrators of the iniquity. The Rajas again invaded Anandpur with a large army; but when notwithstanding their display of valour they were compelled to raise the siege a council of war was held at which they adopted a petition to the Moghul Emperor in which they sought help against the Guru who, said they, had raised a standard of rebellion and was preparing to invade Delhi and avenge his father's assassination by driving out the Moghuls from the Imperial capital.

The latter part of Aurangzebe's life was spent in quelling disturbances in the different parts of his dominions. The policy of distrust and blind fanaticism had created for him numberless foes among the Muslims and non-Muslims of Hindustan proper and the Deccan. The despatches of his Lieutenants in the Punjab, describing the seriousness of affairs, in that far off province, made him turn in his bed. His limited military resources were hardly sufficient to meet the situation nearer home. He knew that the removal of the fighting men, from either the Hindustan or the Deccan, would seriously hamper the operations in which he himself was engaged and would give an occasion to the turbulent spirits, in his dominions, to harass the people. So he very ingeniously contrived a plan which cost him nothing and fully met the requirements of the case. He wrote to the Nawabs of Sirhind and Lahore to march against Anandpur, raze it to the ground and bring the Guru a prisoner to Delhi. Mandates were issued under the royal seal to all defenders of the Faith in the Punjab and its North-West border to crush this rising infidel power. Nawab Mohammad Khan of Maler-Kotla, Usman Khan of Qasur, Shams Khan of Bijwara, Najib Khan of Jullundur and a host of petty chiefs from Jhang, Multan, Bahawalpur and the centres of Gakhar influence, in the country now comprising the districts of Rawalpindi, Attock and Hazara, started with the enthusiasm of the early Christian crusaders, on a holy war against the Guru. They were joined in large numbers by hordes of Rajput hill-men who were not less inimically disposed towards the Sikhs, for their ultra-radicalism and their arrogance in adopting the forms and names which Rajputs alone had assumed from time immemorial. This heterogenous mob, resembling not a little the mob that marched against Jerusalem under the leadership of Peter the Hermit, encamped at the distance of a few miles from Anandpur.

The intelligence of this great and popular campaign against the Guru had spread throughout the land. Bands of Sikh disciples poured in Anandpur from all quarters. Before any engagement took place the Guru had about 10,000 fighting men; but they were neither so well-armed nor so well-equipped. The Imperial army on the other hand is said to have consisted of over a hundred thousand men, mostly used to the troubles and hardships of war. Their disadvantage lay in their diversity of tongues and multiplicity of counsels. The different component parts of the Imperial hosts, though nominally under two or three Generals, looked to their respective leaders for taking the initiative. In this respect the Sikhs were at an advantage. They had one leader whom they obeyed implicitly, through life and death, and who was to them more a god than man.

When the vanguard of the Imperial army was observed from a distance prince Ajit Singh, aided by Said Beg Khan and Mamu Khan, led a band of the Khalsa against the advancing army and gave them battle. The fight was desperate. Both Said Beg Khan and Mamu Khan fell in the action. Several Rajput Rajas and hundreds of Muslim officers and men were killed. The loss of the Sikhs, too, in killed and wounded was not small. But the moral gain was enormous. The Muslims thenceforward were not able to come too near Anandpur. No great battle afterwards took place. Profiting from past experience the Muslim Generals avoided close fights. Anandpur was surrounded on all sides and its communication with the outside world was cut off. The siege lasted for months. Prince Ajit Singh and the Guru's Generals, Daya Singh, Dharm Singh, Sahib Singh, Odai Singh and Alam Singh frequently came out and, both in the dead of night and in the broad light of day, fell upon the Imperial store houses, unawares, and took away large quantities of provisions. But time at length came when this source of supply could not meet requirements. The Guru once made a great effort and himself led out his men against the besieging host; but although the Muslim hordes suffered immensely, the loss was not sufficiently serious to compel the Imperial officers to raise the siege. The protracted operations, however, made them impatient. They took it a serious reflection on their valour that, with a force so large, they should have taken so many months to reduce a 'Faqir' to subjection. In the Imperial despatches, furthermore, they were reprimanded for their incompetency. They knew that if the expedition failed they would be disgraced and exposed to public ridicule. All these considerations compelled them to take Anandpur. Twice they forced an entrance into it by breaking the gates open but were turned out with a tremendous loss. Ladders were prepared and several attempts were made to scale the walls; but the vigilance of the guards, in the fortress of Anandpur, defeated these attempts. At length tired of these manly efforts the Imperial officers had almost determined to raise the siege when the cunning hill Rajas prevailed upon them to employ craft and thus get rid of the hated foe. They represented to the Moghuls that the Sikhs were reduced to the verge of starvation and that they would gladly evacuate Anandpur, if the Imperial authorities guaranteed their safe passage. The proposal was agreed to and communicated to the Guru through a special messenger. When the messenger arrived some of the Sikhs who, unused to war, were yearning for an opportunity to leave Anandpur ran to mother Gujri and entreated her to prevail upon the Guru to yield and thus prevent the annihilation from hunger and thirst of the men who had served him so faithfully. The kind-hearted lady immediately repaired to the Diwan Khana and remonstrated with the Guru for his stubbornness in sticking to a place which had been the cause of so much trouble to her family ever since it was occupied. She proposed moving to Malwa the people of which were mostly adherents of the Guru and where he would have greater freedom in maturing and advancing his schemes. It would be a grievous mistake, said she, to refuse taking advantage of the safe conduct assured by a royal decree and a sheer cruelty to see so many faithful and loving followers die of hunger and suffering.

The Guru refused to listen to the proposal. He told her respectfully that he had no faith in the promises of either the hill Rajputs or of the Turks. The cup of iniquity of both these aggressive people had become full and time was not distant when they would be punished for their misdeeds. He knew that the besieging Generals had become tired of continuing their operations, and he was confident that if the Sikhs patiently bore the difficulties for a few days more, the siege would be raised and all trouble would then be over. But the speech was not at all consoling to the mother who left the Guru in anger saying that if he persisted in his obstinate course not one Sikh would remain with him.

No sooner she left, the Guru sent for his followers and told them that they were free to go if they consented to disown him as their Guru and subscribed their names to a document, thereafter remembered as 'Beda'wa.' Most of them, reduced to mere skeletons, by starvation and disease, took this desperate step and thus escaped to their homes. Some were still left who even then had not the courage to abandon their Guru. They assured him that they had devoted themselves to him, body and soul, and that death with him was dearer to them than life without him. But death from starvation is the most terrible of all deaths. With the exception of a very small number all of them again approached mother Gujri and repeated their previous prayer, and when in reply to her statement that she had no control over her son they proposed to her that she and the Guru's wife and sons might leave Anandpur, she gave her consent disregardful of the Guru's wishes, believing that by so doing she would save the lives of the members of her family as also of the Sikhs who were equally dear to her.

The Guru's feelings, when he learnt of the preparations for departure, in defiance of his wishes, can well be imagined. Finding his authority, thus set at naught, he, too, arranged to accompany his family and followers, though even then he could not help saying that the step taken was suicidal and that if they had waited a couple of days more the trouble would have been over. In all haste the ladies and children, provided with such valuables as could be removed, were placed in chariots. Of the Pyaras and other faithful warriors some posted themselves in the front and others at the back while the Guru and his select Lieutenants protected the flanks. The party marched in this order. When it had fairly got out the perfidious Muslim Generals, instigated by Raja Ajmere Chand, ordered an assault. The Sikhs returned the fire. Prince Ajit Singh stopped to face the enemy and, for a while, prevented their advance which enabled the Guru to cover a distance of some miles. But though reinforcements arrived, the small party of the Sikhs was over-powered by the myriads of the Imperial army. Some were killed and wounded. Others fled in all directions and were subsequently killed by the vindictive hill population. A few, among whom were the Guru and his family, retreated in the direction of Chamkaur; but their progress was impeded by the hill torrent Sirsa. Meantime the royal army came upon them. Resistance being impossible the Guru, with his two sons, Ajit Singh and Jujhar Singh, plunged into the river and escaped. His two wives, dressed in male attire, were escorted to Delhi where they found shelter with a disciple named Jowahir Singh. Mother Gujri, with princes Zorawar Singh and Fateh Singh, who were yet mere children, concealed herself in a cave. Ganga Ram, an old Brahman servant of the family, was in attendance upon her. He offered her the shelter of his house in the village Kheri, a few miles off. Under the circumstances the offer was gladly accepted. The man lodged the lady and her two grandsons at his house and deposited the luggage which contained jewelry and other valuables in some secret place.

Guru Govind Singh himself with princes Ajit Singh and Jujhar Singh and a hundred men took the direction of Ropar. In the way the Pathans of Ropar fell upon the party. The Sikhs fought with usual valour with their ancient foe and inflicted a heavy loss on them; but their own number was reduced to forty by the time they reached Chamkaur. As the place where they halted was exposed to the attack of the enemy who were following them closely Gariba, a poor Jat, offered them a shelter in a kinsman's house, built in the shape of a redoubt. It was an offer too good to be refused. Forthwith the party repaired there and with the help of the villagers attended to necessary repairs. Early at dawn, the enemy surrounded the redoubt. The Sikhs, profiting from the night's rest, fought like lions. Their arrows spread terror into the ranks of the enemy. At length, when ammunition and provisions were exhausted and no hope of escape except an ignominous surrender was left, Prince Ajit Singh, who was hardly seventeen years old, begged leave to emerge from the fortress and die fighting. The request was granted. With Mohkam Singh Pyara, Ishwar Singh, Lal Singh, Nand Singh, Kesra Singh, Mohr Singh and half a dozen more Sikhs Prince Ajit Singh left the redoubt and with a sword in hand and the name of the Timeless One on his lips he fell upon the enemy. The skill and bravery with which he fought drew forth admiration from both sides. Nazim Wazir Khan and Zabardast Khan who were witnessing the fight from an eminence called upon some of their bravest men to engage with the prince and his comrades, in an hand to hand encounter; but none dared advance. The end could not, however, be delayed. Having killed a regular host of the enemy the Prince died a glorious death immortalising his name for all time.

Seeing Prince Ajit Singh die so gloriously his brother, Prince Jujhar Singh, who was not yet fourteen and whose beauty and pleasing manners had made him a universal favourite, approached his father with a request for permission to die likewise. The Guru, pleased at the exhibition of so much courage on the part of his young boy, sent him into the battle-field, beautifully dressed and well armed, with Himmat Singh and Sahib Singh Pyara and half a dozen more valiant disciples. The brave little boy had not proceeded far when feeling his lips parched, all of a sudden, he stopped and asked for a cup of water. "Darling", said the Guru, "angels are awaiting thee with a cup of the water of immortality! Go and take it in the company of thy brother!" The young Prince did not cast another look on those whom he was leaving behind. Inspired with the enthusiasm of the moment he plunged himself into the thick of the fight. Like an eagle he seemed to alight from on high and fall on his prey, when least expected, flying back with equal suddenness and leaving the huge concourse of men looking up helplessly with wonder and dismay. His sprightly feats, performed with the handsome little sword with which his father had provided him, the wondrous movements of his steed, which seemed to move in the ranks of the enemy, more like a spirit than a being of flesh and blood, elicited shouts of applause from the Imperial Generals who would fain have saved his life; but before they could do anything to give effect to this desire all was over. The Prince and his comrades fell to rise no more!.

# CHAPTER XX.

Prince Jujhar Singh departed with the last rays of the departing Sun. The horizon was darkened and just as the great Orb of Heaven while sinking appears to grow bigger and bigger, the illustrious Sikh Leader, notwithstanding that he had lost his equally illustrious sons and many of his brave champions, seemed to be inspired with greater vigour than he ever possessed. The night spread its curtains; but his arrows still pierced many a breast. The bullets from the ramparts still rained death on the men below. The enemy, however, did not seem to mind this fusilade. Elated with joy at the turn the events of the day had taken and confident in the belief that, in the morning following, they would either kill the Guru or take him a prisoner to Delhi they stopped fighting and ordering a small detachment to keep guard they retired to their tents to take the night's repose.

The non chalance of the Moghuls suggested the idea of escape to the Pyaras Dharm Singh and Daya Singh and Bhai Man Singh. They prevailed upon the Guru to leave Bhai Sangat Singh, Kehr Singh, Santokh Singh, Dewa Singh, Ram Singh, Jeewan Singh and Katha Singh in charge of the fortress and suggested that he should himself escape attended by them. At the dead of night when all was quiet outside the redoubt the Guru and his three attendants escaped eluding the vigilance of the guard. The night was pitch-dark. Except the stentorian voice of the sentinels not a sound was audible. The party had not gone far off when the advance guard catching the sound of footsteps and suspecting that it must be the fugitives from the redoubt sounded their horns. The whole camp was disturbed. Men rushed to and fro. Friends killed friends and in the confusion thus caused the Guru and his attendants were separated. At dawn he reached the outskirts of village Kheri. Alfu and Gamu, Gujjars, who were grazing their cattle in the field recognised him and retarded his progress. When even the gift of a few pieces of gold failed to secure their good-will the Guru put them to the sword. In the vicinity of Bahlolpur the Sun rose. Espying a dense cluster of trees the Guru laid himself down under their shade. No water was within sight. He quenched his thirst with the juice of the leaves of the 'Aq' plant, and partly on account of the intoxicating influence of this juice and chiefly on account of intense fatigue he fell in a swoon. At nightfall on regaining consciousness he endeavoured to resume his journey; but his strength failed. He had made up the distance from Chamkaur bare-footed. The rough and thorny paths had lacerated his limbs. He had not proceeded far off when his legs refused to work. Lying on the grass, when blood was flowing profusely from his limbs, when hunger and thirst were tormenting him he invoked the spirits above to go and convey to the Divine Preceptor this tidings of him, his disciple. "Dear friend", says he in the hymn, " where Thou art not, there soft beds are to me like disease; residence in mansions like living among serpents ; wine bottles like the cross ; wine cups like the sword ; all this like death from a butcher's knife ! Indeed my Friend's turf is better, far better! Cursed be residence in palaces!" In this manner he passed the night singing the glory of the Lord of Hosts and remembering Him in words expressing the greatest gratitude. A few hours before dawn, refreshed by the night's breeze and feeling some strength he took the direction of Malwa. At daybreak he sank again, from sheer exhaustion, at a garden, in the suburbs of Machhiwara. As the Providence would have it the Pyaras Dharm Singh, Daya Singh and Bhai Man Singh arrived at the same garden in their search for the Guru. Learning from some one working in the garden, that a person dressed like them was lying in another part of the garden they proceeded thither. To their intense joy they recognised their Guru in the man that lay prostrate before them. Slowly and noiselessly they approached him and kissed his feet. The Guru laid his hand on his sword believing it must be the touch of enemies; but when his eyes opened and he saw his beloved followers, kneeling before him, the momentary rigidity of his countenance gave place to a radiant smile. They drew out thorns from his feet and clothes, and Man Singh, placing him on his back, took him to a well close by and there attended to his bath.

Meantime Ghani Khan and Nabi Khan, Rohilla Pathans, who were the masters of the garden, and from whom the Guru had purchased horses several times, arrived at the spot. Seeing him in such a plight they were moved to tears and then and there vowed that they would do all in their power to serve him and would die with him, if need be. Gulaba Masand, too, on hearing of the Guru's presence in the garden came to pay his respects and brought food for the Guru and his attendants.

A short while after the Guru was removed to a room in the upper storey of the Masand's house. No sooner this was done the Imperial army surrounded the village. Before, however, they could institute any search for him the Guru dressed himself in blue and in this guise succeeded in making his escape through the kind offices of Ghani Khan and Nabi Khan.

At two days' distance from Machhiwara when the danger of pursuit by the Imperial soldiery was over Ghani Khan and Nabi Khan were sent back to their homes rewarded with *Hukmnamas* ordering all disciples to recognize their faithful service. When he arrived at the village of Alamgir, by slow marches, a brother of the famous Bhai Mani Singh offered a beautiful horse which the Guru accepted. Resuming the journey on horse back he met Rai Kalla, a Muslim Chieftain. This man was a Rajput convert. The Guru's story drew tears from his eyes and so strong was his emotion that he would not permit him to proceed further unless he honoured his abode and tasted his food. The invitation was accepted.

At night at the instance of the Guru, a messenger named Mahi, was sent to Sirhind to bring tidings of the Guru's family and followers. Mahi, next day, brought the intelligence that Gangu Brahman, when escorting mother Gujri to his native village, found out that the mule carrying princes Zorawar Singh and Fateh Singh was laden with gold and jewelry. From his childhood upwards he had worked in the Guru's kitchen and had lived on the Guru's bounty. The immense wealth he was carrying turned his head. "How easy it is," thought he, "to appropriate all this. Now this life of drudgery is over. The remainder of my days, O luck! I shall pass in ease and comfort!" Arriving at his house he concealed the jewelry somewhere. Late in the night he cried out "Thief! Thief!" Mother Gujri had passed a sleepless night. She had not seen any stranger in the room. Only Gangu had been there several times. "Dear boy", said she to Gangu, "no thief has come here. I have been awake all this while. Pray do not make noise. Take possession of all the jewelry and enjoy it as best as thou mayst. Thou hast been brought up in our house and it would be, indeed, a pleasure to me, if the jewelry should fall into thy hands rather than into those of the Moghals. But pray do not invite a crowd here. People will recognise us and the cruel Turks will not spare the lives of my boys." The traitor, pretending to have been insulted, accused the lady of ingratitude. He had rescued her and the young princes from the clutches of death and for this he was rewarded by being called a thief. Immediately he placed the lady and the princes in the custody of the Muslim authorities who transferred them to Wazir Khan, Subah of Sirhind. This bigot, disregarding the ages of the princes, who were yet mere children, offered them the option of the *Kalima* or the sword. They preferred the latter. After subjecting them to nameless tortures the monster ordered their being bricked up alive. When the wall reached the waists of the princes they were again asked to accept Islam, so that their lives might be spared; but they refused to yield. "We are," said they, "sons of Guru Govind Singh. What is death to us? We must die in order that the wrongs of Aryavarta may be avenged. So, miscreant, let thy craving for blood be satiated." Nawab Sher Mohammad Khan of Malerkotla interceded for the young princes; but Sucha Nand Khatri, Minister of the Nawab of Sirhind, was not in favour of sparing their lives. In his opinion they were young cobras and deserved to be treated as such. Wazir Khan was only too glad to accept his Minister's suggestion. He nodded to the public executioner. The order was forthwith obeyed and so in the presence of a vast multitude the heads of the princes were cut off. When the intelligence of this atrocious crime was conveyed to mother Gujri she threw herself out of the window of the dungeon and falling on the ground below expired immediately. The disciples became frantic with grief. Their loud lamentations were heard throughout the land and men saw that the day of retribution was not far off.

Taking leave of Rai Kalla the Guru travelled from village to village in Malwa. When he arrived at Deena, Lakhmir, Samir and Takht Mal, grandsons of Rai Jodha who had helped Guru Har Govind in obtaining victory over the Moghal Generals, Lal Beg Khan and Karm Khan, at the battle of Guru Sar, came to pay their respects to him. The brothers vied with one another in serving the Guru and his attendants. Their love and devotion prolonged the Guru's stay there. From all parts of the country people flocked to the place to pay their respects to him. The greater part of his time he spent in preaching God's word to them and in inculcating the principles of fellow-feeling and sacrifice. His sermons, imbued with heavenly fervour, his account of the heroic deeds of the Sikhs during the siege of Anandpur, his reference to the martyrdom of princes Ajit Singh and Jujhar Singh and to the bold manner in which princes Zorawar Singh and Fateh Singh met death at Sirhind were listened to with the deepest attention. The very souls of the hearers were stirred.

The large mustering of men at Deena alarmed Wazir Khan. A messenger brought a "Parwana" in which the Subah charged Lakhmir and Samir with sheltering an enemy of the Emperor and threatened them with condign punishment if they did not immediately deliver him to the authorities. Lakhmir and Samir returned the messenger with the reply that they had done no wrong in serving their Guru and that instead of delivering him to his enemies they would sacrifice their homes and hearths, nay their very lives, for his sake, when time came.

Finding that the time was arriving when another battle would have to be fought with his old foe, the Subah of Sirhind, the Guru issued a proclamation calling upon all fighting men among his disciples to come and enlist in the army he was raising. In a few days a large number of brave Barars, a clan of Jats, offered themselves for service, and thus the

Guru again had a regular force for service in time of emergency.

At this time he wrote an epistle to Aurangzebe in which he described the circumstances under which instigated by his officers, the Raja of Bilaspur and the confederate hill chieftains, he had waged an unprovoked war against him, causing immense loss of life and resulting in no good to the Empire. To gain an advantage over him the meanest subterfuges had been resorted to and even oaths on the Quran had not been respected. Did His Majesty think that the Great Protector of the world would leave such misdeeds unpunished? The mission of the Gurus whose *Gaddi* he was adorning was that of peace. Neither he nor his illustrious predecessors had any ambition for acquiring temporal sway over men. His only aim was to instil the fear of God into men's minds and to point out to them the advantages of righteous living. But blinded by prejudice and worldly authority neither His Majesty nor His officers would rest content until a law-abiding people, driven to desperation, took up arms and put an end to his iniquitous rule.

# CHAPTER XXI

During the Guru's travels in Malwa, Sodhi Kaul, a descendant of Prithi Rai, paid him a visit. The blue garments that the Guru still wore no longer served any useful purpose. So when Sodhi Kaul presented him a white suit of clothes the blue ones were cast off and torn into pieces. When asked to explain his action he said that blue cloth was the symbolic representation of Islamic influence. Baba Nanak had blessed Babar with the rule of Hindustan for seven generations. The period specified was closing and in tearing the blue dress he was only making this announcement. The Moghuls had made themselves a scourge and the interests of humanity demanded that the sceptre of Government be wrested from them.

Chaudhri Kapura was an influential Jat and owner of a hundred villages. Pyara Dharm Singh asked him, on behalf of the Guru, to allow the accupation of his fortified village of Kot Kapura. The man refused the request. He failed to understand the reasonableness of offering further opposition to Moghul arms, shut up in a tiny village like Kot Kapura, when the fortifications of Anandpur had proved of no avail. Moreover, he had no mind to consent to an undertaking that would be tantamount to rebellion against the authority of the Moghul Emperor. He had a great stake in the country and he was not prepared to lose his vast property and meet death at the hands of a hangman. This coarse reply offended the Sikhs. The man left the assembly in disgrace and, curiously enough, as fate would have it, he was hanged, not long after, by the order of Isa Khan, a neighbouring Muslim Rajput, with whom he had a dispute of long standing. His son Sukhiya and gandson Hamira lost no time in tendering an apology for the insolence of their father and offered themselves to be baptised. For this penitent act Hamira received the blessing that his descendants would rule over that part of the country. The present Raja of Farid Kot is a lineal descendant of this Hamira.

Sodhi Kaul, finding that baptised Jats were so highly honoured by the Guru and the Panth and thinking that a Sodhi, when baptised, would acquire a far superior rank in the estimation of the believers had Abhai Chand, a grandson of his, also baptised to the new Faith. This person, thenceforward known by the name of Abhai Singh, always posed as a Guru and gave no end of trouble on account of his extreme greed and selfishness.

The Manjha Sikhs who had deserted the Guru at Anandpur and had disowned him were, in their turn, disowned by their people, on their return home. Their wives told them to wear female attire and stay at home, while the women would go and fight for the Guru. So public hatred as well as self-mortification, led them to seek for a reconciliation with the Guru. With this view forty penitent souls went to Malwa to have an audience with the Guru and pray for forgiveness. The Guru's army lay encamped in the outskirts of a wood. Espying the Moghul forces advancing towards it from a distance they entrenched themselves behind a cluster of trees that grew around a small pool of water and resolved to give their lives for the sake of the Guru, then and there. When the Muslims came within shot, bullets and arrows from the bushes retarded their progress. Believing that this was the mass of the Sikh force the enemy did not approach near enough; but after some hours' fighting they were emboldened to come to close quarters. The brave band fought like lions, and though infinitesimally small in number, they died to a man, inflicting heavy losses on the enemy. The heat was intense and the country waterless. Both man and beast panted for breath. Immediately the aspect of the heavens changed. A strong wind began to blow in the face of the invaders. Clouds of sand rose high in the air and seemed to be determined on burying the marauding hosts alive. The horizon was darkened. Not a soul could be distinguished. Fearing annihilation the Subah of Sirhind ordered a retreat without engaging the main body of the Sikh army.

The defence of the pass of Thermopylæ by a small band of Spartans under Leonidas is not more proudly and more gratefully remembered by Hellenic peoples than the gallantry which these forty men displayed in opposing the progress of thousands of disciplined warriors in an open country, wanting even in a pretence of defence. There is no Sikh home, no Sikh temple, where, up to this day, the Sikh devotee does not admiringly remember the "Forty Saved Ones". The story is pathetically told that when after the retreat of the royal army the Guru visited the place of action he saw mother Bhago, prince Zorawar Singh's nurse, washing her wounds. She it was that had taunted the men for their previous defection. She it was that had brought them back to atone for their sin by offering their lives for their country and their Guru and had led the attack on the advancing foe. Among the heaps of the slain the Guru recognised his disciples. Lifting them, one by one, and placing their heads on his thigh, he wiped their faces with his kerchief, kissed them, calling them by their names and praising them for their unprecedented valour, as if they were alive and were hearing his loving remembrances. While he was thus engaged his hands fell upon one Mahan Singh in whom life was not yet extinct. The man's delight knew no bounds at the sight of the Saviour holding him in his embrace. The Guru, too, was equally filled with joy at the opportunity thus afforded of exchanging a few words with one of the devoted band of heroes. He enquired if the dying man had a wish which he desired to be fullfilled. "*Tuti gáhndo*". "Unite the broken tie" was the reply. He believed the Guru to be the image of the Most High and Just. As the Providence forgave penitent sinners, he prayed that the Guru might be graciously pleased to forgive him and his comrades for their having abandoned him at Anandpur. The Saviour was moved to tears. Forthwith he took out the "*Bedáwa*" from his pocket and tore it into pieces, thus convincing the dying hero that the signatories to the document were thenceforward forgiven. Mahan Singh shed tears of joy and expired in the Guru's lap. No wonder, then, that the spot should have been, thereafter, remembered Muktsar (Tank of Salvation) and should have become one of the chief places of pilgrimage.

# CHAPTER XXII.

So long as the Guru was at Anandpur it was never found necessary to pay the disciples for service rendered. Men and women, highly respected in society, considered it an act of merit to perform even the meanest duties in the Guru's household. When war was proclaimed against him the disciples ran to him, armed and equipped at their own expense and provided with sufficient stores and ammunition for their use. But when the Guru was compelled to leave Anandpur and retire to Malwa the uncertainty of his movements made it difficult for the disciples, in the remote provinces, to make themselves useful to him. He had thenceforward to depend mostly on the Malwa Jats. When he found it necessary to raise an army in Malwa to oppose the advance of the Imperial forces under the Subah of Sirhind he had, for the first time, to introduce the system of paid service. His resources, at this time, were, however, not considerable. The pay of the men fell in arrears. The result was that they became turbulent and refractory and, if a disciple from the North-West frontier had not timely arrived, with a mule load of gold and silver coins, it would have been difficult to maintain discipline. The trouble being thus over the paid troops were immediately disbanded. Only a small number of disciples remained who formed a volunteer force, under Dan Singh, a devoted follower, resident of a village in the neighbourhood of Kot Bhai, in the Ferozepore district.

Syad Wahmi, a Muslim Faqir of great renown in those parts, was baptised to the Sikh Faith and named Ajmere Singh. His name is frequently mentioned in the Sikh annals; and it is stated that he was one of the few who accompanied the Guru to the Deccan and rendered him conspicuous service. Such conversions, though rare, afford sufficient evidence to show that Muslims were taken into the Sikh fold and were given the same status as was possessed by converts from amongst the Hindus. This conversion serves as an illustration of the Guru's catholicity and shows that Sikhism is a proselytising creed and is not exclusive as Hinduism.

Notwithstanding the general belief that the Government of the day was against the Guru and his propaganda he still continued to obtain adherents from amongst the influential land-holders and Jagirdars of Malwa. Of these chieftains Rai Dalla, of Talwandi Sabo, now known as Damdama Sahib, was the foremost. He placed all his vast resources at the disposal of the Guru and became an enthusiastic champion of his cause. This alarmed Wazir Khan, Subah of Sirhind. He sent several threatening orders to the Rai calling upon him to beware of harbouring a foe of the Emperor. The threats proved of no avail. The Rai wrote in reply that the Guru was his spiritual lord and master to whom he was bound by most sacred ties and that for no consideration he would be a party to any scheme that aimed at harassing him. Infuriated at this rebuff the Subah again applied to Aurangzebe for assistance in subduing the Guru and the refractory Jat nobles that had taken up his cause.

When the Guru was sharing the hospitality of Rai Dalla his wives Sundri and Sahib Dewi came from Delhi. Since they were taken to the Imperial capital, in male attire, on the occasion of the bloody skirmish that had taken place on the banks of Sirsa, they had received no intelligence concerning the subsequent events. On hearing of the martyrdom of Princes Ajit Singh, Jujhar Singh, Zorawar Singh and Fateh Singh and of the tragic end of mother Gujri they fell senseless on the floor. The large gathering of Sikh ladies and gentlemen who had come to pay their respects to them were filled with grief. The lamentations of the bereaved mothers, when they regained consciousness, drew tears from the eyes of the whole assembly. The Guru, all the while sitting sedate and calm, said to them words of comfort and solace. They were told that their sons were not really dead. They had died to remain alive for all time; for theirs was the death of martyrs for their country and their creed.

The Guru's memory was wonderfully retentive. This was exemplified in his compiling the whole of Ad Granth from memory. He had asked for the original Granth from Baba Dhirmal; but his request was refused with the taunt that when he prided so much on his talents it could not be a difficult matter to him to have a Granth of his own. Now when the Guru was free from the worries and anxieties of war he reproduced the whole volume from memory.

When the epistle referred to in Chapter XXI was delivered personally to Aurangzebe by Pyara Daya Singh he was deeply impressed by the demeanour of the messenger and by the ability and pathos the writing displayed. A bigot though he was he could not conceal from himself the fact that at the instigation of the hill Rajas his officers in the Punjab had unnecessarily involved themselves into a quarrel with the Guru and had committed wanton excesses which provoked opposition and resulted in so much loss of life. He sent peremptory orders to the Punjab Subahs to stop molesting the Guru any further and let him live where it suited him. In reply to Wazir Khan's request for further reinforcements to chastise the Malwa Jats, for taking up the Guru's cause, he reprimanded the Subah asking him to explain why he had lent support to the hill chieftains in their efforts to crush the growing influence of the Guru and had unnecessarily provoked popular opposition to the Muslim rule. He sent a special messenger to the Guru asking him to come and see him so that he might have an opportunity of making amends for what had happened. Though warned by many a disciple for placing any reliance on the treacherous old monarch the Guru accepted the invitation. The ladies were again sent to Delhi. With a reduced following the Guru immediately afterwards started for the Deccan where Aurangzebe was then engaged in quelling disturbances.

# CHAPTER XXIII.

While the Guru was on his way to the Deccan intelligence arrived of the death of Aurangzebe. This did not deter him from prosecuting the journey. He had a desire to visit Rajputana and preach his doctrines in this land of heroes; but he had hardly set his foot on the Rajput territory when a messenger from prince Muazzam arrived which led to a change of his plans. The usual sanguinary strife that invariably took place among the claimants to the throne on the death of an Asiatic sovereign divided the Moghul counsels. Prince Azam with the help of the army had himself proclaimed Emperor. Prince Muazzam, the eldest son, was at Kabul at the time of Aurangzebe's death. He, too, assumed regal honours and, under the title of Bahadar Shah, marched to Delhi to contest the throne. He sent his Minister, Diwan Nand Lal, to the Guru praying for assistance in the prosecution of his design. Diwan Nand Lal was a favourite disciple of the Guru. His mission was, therefore, successful. The Guru assured him of his sympathy and forthwith issued orders to the disciples in the whole Punjab and the frontier summoning them to Agra. In response to the summons the Sikhs mustered in force. Their command was entrusted to Pyara Daya Singh. In the battle that ensued the combatants fought bravely: but when the partisans of prince Muazzam, merely on account of the smallness of number, were giving way, the Guru's arrow, it is said, killed prince Azam. His death was a signal of flight to his army. At a Durbar, held next day, in the fort of Agra, Bahadar Shah was duly proclaimed Emperor. On this occasion he was presented with *Nazars* by all men of might and influence in the land. He availed himself of that opportunity to publicly acknowledge his gratitude to the Guru. The Sikh officers and men were handsomely rewarded. This done he took leave of the Guru and left for Delhi. A court notable was appointed who remained in attendance on the Guru. According to Kahfi Khan, " at the time that Bahadar Shah marched towards Hyderabad the Chief Guru of this sect came to join him with two or three hundred horsemen*." For what purpose the Guru joined Bahadur Shah Kahfi Khan does not say. But bearing all things in mind one feels strongly persuaded to believe in the Sikh version of the affair and to regard the attentions of Bahadur Shah as an expression of a feeling of gratefulness or, what is not very unlikely, the Moghul Emperor might have been prompted by the ordinary dictates of policy in honouring the Guru, as he did, and kept him in close touch with himself; for a formidable foe, removed from his sphere of influence, becomes quite harmless, in the nature of things. Leaving Agra and passing through Mathra, Brinda Ban and Gokal, places of historic renown, the Guru arrived at Delhi and encamped in the spacious lawns of Moti Bagh. The Emperor was assiduous in his attentions to him.

Seeing Bahadur Shah firmly established on the throne, the Guru asked him to conciliate his Hindu

---

* *Vide* History of India, as told by its own historians, by Sir H. M. Elliot, K.C.B. Volume VII.

and Sikh subjects by ordering the abandonment of the policy of forcibly converting people to Islam and chastising his Lieutenants in the provinces whose outrageous conduct had provoked rebellion all round.

The Emperor did not feel himself sufficiently strong to comply with the demand made. He allowed days, weeks and months to pass without doing anything. The Guru must have felt annoyed, when he found that his wishes were not respected by the man who had come to the throne through his own instrumentality. But it appears that the Emperor was able to keep him in good humour ; and when he had fairly succeeded in restoring order at his capital he left for Rajputana to suppress a rebellion of the Rajputs in Jeypore and Marwar. When he was engaged in this occupation the Guru separated from him to pay a visit to Nanded, a small town on the Godaveri. There is no evidence on record to show that, while in the Deccan, the Guru opened communications with the Marhatta chieftains during his sojourn in their country. It may be that improved relations with the Moghul Emperor might have suggested to him the adoption of peaceful ways for the amelioration of his people and avoid a coalition with a people in open revolt against the Moghals ; or he might have quietly lived among the Marhattas with a view to cultivate friendly relations with them in order that he might count upon their assistance in time of emergency. But though he did not live long enough to raise recruits in Maharashtra for service in the Punjab, his conversion of a *Bairagi*, subsequently known in history as Banda, more than outweighed the advantages of a possible alliance with the Rajputs or the Marhattas.

Banda was a great genius of the age. In learning and worldly wisdom, in military valour and religious fervour, few surpassed him. Hearing of the Guru's arrival at Nanded he went to see him and was so deeply impressed with his divine grace that he immediately became his disciple and remained, till death, his very ardent admirer and devoted follower. Commissioned by the Guru to carry on the work of freeing the Punjab from the tyrannous yoke of the Muslims and of the arrogant ruling castes and priestly classes he immediately left for that country. Arriving at a village on the south-eastern frontier of the Province, he issued a manifesto, in the name of the Guru, to the disciples throughout the land to come and muster under his banner. Several Sikh nobles of Malwa responded to the call. Mali Singh and Ali Singh Man, who were in the service of the Subah of Sirhind, deserted him and joined Banda. In a surprisingly short time large bands of Sikhs, thirsting for revenge, assembled in the place of muster. The town of Sirhind was razed to the ground and its fortifications were dismantled. Samana was stormed and pillaged. A detachment of Moghul Horse carrying lacs of rupees was overpowered and the money distributed among the victors. The town of Mustafabad was then besieged and captured. The Mussalmans who had been accustomed to slaughter kine in Hindu quarters and violate the chastity of Hindu girls were put to the sword, and their houses were plundered. Damla, the village of the treacherous Pathans who had deserted the Guru in the battle of Bhangani, was pillaged and plundered. Hundreds of other towns and villages met with a similar fate and the whole Islamic Punjab was struck with terror. In rage Wazir Khan of Sirhind who was mainly responsible for this outburst of revenge marched in force to chastise the marauders. His career was, however, run. Neither he nor his army now inspired respect or fear. He was captured in a pitched battle. His sons and other kinsmen were put to death in his presence and he himself met an ignominous end, too shocking to describe. His Vizir, Sucha Nand, who had urged the murder of princes Zorawar Singh and Fateh Singh, was likewise tortured to death. In this manner most of those who had been guilty of atrocious behaviour were chastised.

Banda himself was foredoomed. He had overstepped the Guru's instructions and flushed with victory had set up a sect of his own which subordinated everything to political craft. The excesses committed by him and the unheeded warnings of the Guru could not go unpunished. To use the words of Talboys Wheeler " the Sikhs were signally defeated and Banda Guru was taken prisoner and conducted to Delhi amidst a horrible procession of eight hundred prisoners doomed to death and two thousand bleeding heads borne on poles. The executions that followed were ghastly and sickening. The Sikh prisoners were beheaded at the rate of a hundred a day. The captive Guru was clothed in mock robes of state and exhibited with an infant son in an iron cage. The child was butchered before his eyes and he himself was tortured to death by hot pincers. But Banda Guru perished in the glory of martyrdom exulting in the dream that he had been raised by God to scourge the sins and oppressions of age."

Bhai Karm Singh, a young Sikh historian who has written a beautiful life of Banda in Punjabi, says that the body of Banda was thrown on the banks of Jamna. Some spark of life was still left. A hermit close by took him to his hut and attended to his wounds. Careful nursing resuscitated him. When able to move about he left Delhi *incognito* and took up his abode on the banks of the Chenab, near the village of Babbar, in the Jummu territory. There he remarried. His descendants are still found there. They have a large following.

Meantime Guru Govind Singh's end drew nigh. One day when he was lecturing on God's love for mankind, irrespective of caste or creed, clime or country, and was attacking the creeds which legalised persecution of the peoples different in faith he was stabbed by a Pathan fanatic. The wound was immediately stitched and, in a few months, the Guru was able to move about and attend to his usual programme of work. Unfortunately, however, before the wound was quite healed he stretched a huge bow at an athletic tournament. The effort was too much for an invalid. The stitches of the wound broke asunder and blood flowed profusely. When he saw that his strength was failing and his dissolution was approaching he collected his disciples and told them to regard the Principle in the *Granth Sahib* as their Guru, thenceforward, and to submit other matters of moment to an assembly of five representative elders and abide by their decision. He told them to worship only the one Lord of Lords and to lead temperate and useful lives. Thus strengthening the belief of the disciples in the tenets of his creed and exhorting them to receive all calamities with resignation the Saviour passed away. His dissolution took place at the age of forty-two, in 1708 A. D., according to *Samvat* 1765 Vikrimaditya, on Sudi 5th, Kartik, at midnight. His body was cremated and the ashes were buried at a spot where now stands the *Gurudwara* of Hazur Sahib, or Abchala Nagar, situated at Nanded, in the territory of the Nizam of Hyderabad. The *Gurudwara* is principally maintained on the income of a *Jagir* from the Nizam's Government. Railway communication has been opened now with Nanded. The number of visitors to the *Gurudwara* is, therefore, increasing yearly. Maharaja Sir Krishna Prashad, Prime Minister of Hyderabad, and a lineal descendant of Chandu Shah of historic renown, is the leading Sikh in that part of the country and the grant of the *Jagir* for the maintenance of the *Gurudwara* is due mainly to the influence of the Maharaja's family in the State of Hyderabad.

Various accounts are given of the manner in which Guru Govind Singh met with his death. Khafi Khan merely says that the Guru "died from the wounds of a dagger and his murderer was not discovered." The author of *Sair-ul-Mutakharin*, a later writer, says that "the loss of his children affected

Guru Govind Singh so deeply that he shortly after died of grief." The majority of the writers of the Sikh chronicles, on the other hand, hold that the Guru never died. According to them the Guru disappeared as soon as he seated himself on the funeral pyre and was subsequently seen, riding his favourite steed, clad as a warrior. Some of the less credulous say that the Guru had two Pathan lads in his employ whose father he had killed in a battle and who, filled with a feeling of revenge, stole one night into his bed room and stabbed him when he lay asleep. Others more ingenious state that the Guru constantly told these Pathans that those who did not revenge their father's death were cowards and poltroons and thus he actually incited them to assassinate him. This is simply attributing to the Guru the thoughts of a suicide. According to other accounts the Guru was murdered by the secret agents of Emperor Bahadur Shah who, though outwardly friendly, secretly conspired to get rid of a powerful foe, in as quiet a manner as possible, an explanation which thoroughly accords with the admitted blood-thirsty instincts of the later Moghul Emperors. It is a fact that on the receipt of the news of the fall of Sirhind, Samana and Mustafabad, Bahadar Shah suspended operations in the Deccan and led an army in person to put down the Sikh rebellion. He might have been under the impression that Banda was only acting under instructions from the Guru. It does not, therefore, require much effort to imagine that the assassin who put an end to the Guru's earthly existence was an emissary of Bahadur Shah.

# CHAPTER XXIV.

The foregoing pages will show that the Guru passed away when he had hardly attained to ripe manhood. The latter part of his life was mostly taken up by wars and these wars were provoked by his religious and social propaganda. His original idea was to see to the harmonious development of his people through peaceful ways. He believed that if people worshipped one true God and gave up man-hatred and learnt to be loving and sacrificing the problem of their regeneration would solve itself ; but very soon he felt it necessary to arm his followers in self-defence. The conservative Hindu Rajas of the hills in whose territory he started work had got accustomed to religious, social and political slavery, from time immemorial. At first they regarded the Guru's following as a contemptible rabble ; but when, at length, their eyes were opened and they saw the merest dregs of society calling themselves lions and assuming airs of superiority; when they saw their prejudices disregarded and their time-honoured caste distinctions seriously threatened ; when they saw their authority set at naught by a class of men whom they had been hitherto accustomed to tread under their feet ; their susceptibilities were wounded and they invented excuses to resort to violence. But their threats and menaces and military operations against the Guru lent increased vigour to the new movement. The Guru was firmly convinced that the prevailing religion of the time was incapable of infusing vitality into the inert mass of humanity which inhabited this country. Its multiplicity of creeds, its countless gods and myriads of objects of worship had removed people from the worship of the one great Lord who alone was the source of all good. This rebellion against the Lord of the Universe was at the root of all evil*. Hindu Society had further lost its elasticity. Adaptation to changed order of things, liberty of conscience, and expansive morality were unknown to the Hindus. Their transcendental philosophy and their boasted literature had failed to instil love for their fellow-men into their minds. Each individual lived for himself. Such a thing as coalition against common danger was unknown to them. The scriptures had been so moulded and so interpreted as to make the vast Indian population believe that the best thing that they could do was to serve the Brahmans and thus to attain beatitude in this life and that to come. Thus the great mass of Indian humanity was kept by its own leaders in eternal, intellectual, spiritual and political bondage without knowing, perhaps, that such a course would lead not only to the gradual demoralization of the great majority of their countrymen, but to their own downfall, as it eventually did.

How truly the writer of a communicated article, headed "The Struggle for Freedom," in the Lahore *Tribune*, dated November 3rd, 1906, expresses himself in this connection :—

"Politics, Religion, Science, and Sociology are so inextricably mixed up together that it is

---

* Parmeshar te bhulliáu viyápan sabhe rog.

impossible to say where one ends and the other begins. Turn which way you like religion stares you in the face. Professor Huxley said that whatever path he pursued in science he came across the everlasting notice board "No Thoroughfare"—by order of Moses. The struggles for scientific truths have been bitter and immense. The ecclesiastics have in the history of the world wielded an immense power. Kingdoms have been made and kingdoms have been given away in the name of religion. The teachers of religions have always lived on the fat of the land, and in return for the munificent gifts by pious devotees they have taught them obedience to themselves, charity which invariably is exercised in their favour, by donation of lands, houses, jewels, money —and hatred of other sects, which has been the cause of so much bloodshed in the past, and of the degradation of whole communities in our own times. How the Roman Catholics hate the Protestants with a bitter hatred in the name of the Lord they both worship! How the Sunnis hate the Shiahs in the name of the Prophet they both acknowledge! The Mukalids hate the *gair* Mukalids! How the Brahmin despises the Sudra and how he has by minutely detailed laws kept the Sudra down in intelligence and knowledge only to serve his own selfish ends! Religion has made divine laws to keep one community strictly separated from another. The laws of Moses were very strict on the subject. In Deuteronomy (Ch. VII) it is written "And when the Lord thy God shall deliver them before thee, thou shalt smite them and utterly destroy them. Thou shalt make no covenant with them, nor show any mercy unto them. Neither shalt thou make marriage with them. Thy daughter thou shalt not give unto his son nor his daughter shalt thou take unto your son. For thou art an holy people unto the Lord thy God." Manifestly, then, the mighty Jehovah of the Jews was a tribal God and not a God of Universal Brotherhood as preached by Christ 1,500 years later. The laws of Manu are perhaps unequalled by any thing of a like nature in the world for their severity, inequality, injustice and cruelty. In Chapter I, it is thus written:— "For the sake of *preserving this universe the Being*, supremely glorious, allotted separate duties to those who sprang respectively from his mouth, his arms, his thigh and his foot. To Brahmins he assigned the duties of reading the Vedas, of teaching it, of sacrificing, of assisting others to sacrifice, of giving alms if they be rich and if indigent of receiving gifts. To defend the people, to give alms, to sacrifice, to read the Veda, to shun the allurements of sensual gratification, are in a few words the duties of Kshatrya. To keep herds of cattle, to bestow largesses, to sacrifice, to read the scriptures, to carry on trade, to lend on interest and to cultivate land are permitted to a Vaishya." One principal duty the Supreme Ruler assigned to a Sudra, namely, to serve the classes above mentioned. Here we have a law, under the sanction of the Supreme Ruler of the Universe, which divides God's people into four distinct classes, and the last class were born only to serve in a menial capacity the twice born classes. Could there be any law more unjust, more partial and more cruel? Could a Sudra join hands with any other class to form a nation? Is there any community of interest in a born slave and his cruel master? The teachings of History are clear and definite on the point that no priest-ridden people have ever developed into a nation. The priests for their own selfish ends will not allow the intellect to expand and have its natural growth. It is cramped and distorted from its infancy and is never given an opportunity to free itself from the trammels of their doctrines and dogmas. The struggle for freedom obviously then is a struggle for freedom of the intellect from the chains of religious ideas. Mazzinni in his message to the Italian workmen said:—"In Italy such aspirations of heart can not exist until the Papacy shall be overthrown in the name of the moral law acknowledged as high above all pretended intermediates between God and the people." The whole question of the struggle for freedom resolves itself into one word *Education*. It is only by education that the darkness of ignorance, of religious prejudice, a hatred of fellow creatures under various pretexts can be dispelled. We must convince men that they are all sons of one sole God and bound to fulfil and execute one sole law here on earth, that each of them is bound to live not for himself but for others. The aim of existence is not to be more happy but to make ourselves and others more virtuous. What India needs is a new religion of humanity, which embraces all that is best, truest and brightest in life. To live for others and not for self, is the greatest happiness of each of us as it is our plain and simple duty. The very end of life is to press onwards ever to a higher state, towards a truer sense of duty for each of us, a purer form of life for our human kind. We should acknowledge that in humanity is gathered up all that is abiding in the past, active in the present, and of promise in the future of man—the worship of one true God of universal brotherhood, of universal equality, and of universal freedom."

This is exactly the Guru's ideal. His God is not a Hindu God, not a Muslim, Jewish or Christian God; but God of Christ, of Ram Mohan Roy, of Keshab Chandar Sen, of Moulana Rum, of Shams Tabrez—in a word, one True God, to Whom whole humanity is alike, Who has created it, feels for it and provides for it, and "Who," to use his own words, "has no name, no home, no caste, no features, no colour, no lineaments. Who is the Primeval Being, Embodiment of generosity, Unborn, the First Essence and Impenetrable. Who has no country, no national costume, no distinctive complexion, shape or bias, and Who here, there, and everywhere permeates and appears in the form of Love."*

The Guru had come into the world to inaugurate the reign of righteousness and to suppress chicanery and fraud in any form. He, therefore, disregarded

---

* Nám thám na ját jákar rúp rang na rekh.
Ád Purkh Udár Múrat Ájon Ád Asekh.
Des aur na bhes jákar rúp rekh na rág.
Jatra tatra dishá vishá hoe phailio anurág.
Jáp ji, stanza 79.

the threats of the hill chieftains and preached open revolt from error. Both in public and in private he condemned man-worship and image-worship in the boldest possible manner. In his famous epistle to Aurangzebe he said that he was a messenger of the Most High sent into the world to put down rebellion from God's authority. The Rajput Rajas of the hills on whose representations the Imperial officers in the Punjab had persecuted him were his foes; because they were worshippers of images, while he was an image-breaker. This explains why he condemned all religious systems which led people astray from the Divine Being and why he set up a creed of his own, called the Khalsa Panth (Pure Way). Into his fold he invited all, Brahmans and Sudras, the proud nobles and the humble serfs, and united them by the ties of a common brotherhood. He did not confine education and religious culture to any particular section of the community. All were free to aspire to the highest rank in society. No one was deprived of the solace of religion because of his low origin. Hope was held out to all that God lifts all who seek His aid.*

This was the gospel brought by the blessed Saviour. Regarded as the representative of God on the Earth, he held out a helping hand to the humble and the lowly. But this ministration of beneficence was short-lived. A great creed that produced Rishis and made "hawks of sparrows" was smothered, as it were, in its infancy. Its tenets had not yet been promul-

* "Jite sharn ai hain tite rákh lai hain."

gated long enough when a protracted war ensued and amidst its excitement all else was forgotten. It is, no doubt, true that at the daily congregations, presided over by the Saviour, the disciples were taught the worship of the One Great Lord; but it is too much to expect that amid the worries and cares of war he could have given sufficient attention to his varied programme of reform. Unfortunately, for this reason, the Guru has not left a complete memoir of his own. He has left no code of laws for the Government of the Panth; perhaps, because he did not like to fetter the hands of his disciples and left them free to make laws for themselves according to the requirements of time and place. The Dassam Granth is believed by some to have been written by the Guru himself; but the great majority of modern Gyanis and thinkers are of opinion that it consists of the literary productions of the Guru and of the men of letters who lived at his court. The writings of the Guru and of his men were lost when the Moghul army treacherously fell upon the Guru and the party of his followers, after their evacuation of Anandpur, on the banks of the river Sirsa, and the Sikhs were either slain or scattered. Such manuscripts as were left with the disciples were long after collected by them and the whole volume was called by them Dassam Granth, or the Granth of the 10th Guru. Thus the only book, associated with the Guru's name, does not give a complete account of what he accomplished. The men who lived with him and worked with him and understood his mission passed away, without leaving an account of their doings. Their successors were only inspired with the one feeling of revenge against Mussalmans as a class. It occurred to nobody that it was the Hindu Rajas of the hills who had excited Muslim fanaticism against the Guru and his work, that Sucha Nand, a Khatri Minister of the Nawab of Sirhind, was mainly responsible for the bricking up alive of princes Zorawar Singh and Fateh Singh, the Guru's two younger sons. Nobody considered the fact that it was respectable Muslims that had helped the Guru in making his escape from the Mughal camp at Machhiwara. All that the people remembered was that the Muslims were the sole cause of the Guru's troubles and of the premature death of his two elder and the murder of his two younger sons. This was enough to excite the worst passions of the community. A wave of anti-Muslim feeling spread throughout the land, causing havoc and destruction and ultimately removing every vestige of the Muslim supremacy in the Punjab. And when this result was achieved to the ordinary Sikh mind the mission of the Khalsa was accomplished. The problems of vaster significance and lasting benefit, the reconstruction of the social system of the community on a just basis, the readjustment of their relations with other fellowmen on humanitarian principles were thenceforward made subservient to matters political.

# CHAPTER XXV.

Talk what some people may about the superior civilization of ancient India, a little examination of such fragmentary knowledge as we possess of the state of society that obtained even in the most palmy days of the Indian civilization establishes beyond question that all learning was confined to a very small privileged class. The great majority of the population, deeply sunk in ignorance, had got accustomed, from time immemorial, to look to this class for guidance in all matters. Their feelings were not their own; their thoughts not their own; and their beliefs not their own. Worshippers of elements, at first, in time they became worshippers of men, at whose bidding they put an end to the lives of their own benefactors and frustrated the efforts that were made, from time to time, to rescue them from the iron-grip of a clique that, not unlike vampires, had suck their very blood out of them and had reduced them to the position of serfs. It is impossible not to admire the feeling which prompted Rama to relinquish the honours of sovereignty and prefer long sojourn in the wilds of Central and Northern India in order that the promise given by his aged sire might be fulfilled. But it is difficult to justify so much bloodshed in the war that he waged against Rawan, whom the gifted Kali Das himself describes as a renowned Brahman and whose only fault seems to have been that he revenged a wanton insult to his sister and that he espoused the cause of the unfortunate aboriginal tribes who were slow to perceive any beauty in the aggressive religion and civilization of our conquering Aryan ancestors. The author of the Mahabharatha himself throws no small blame on Sri Krishnaji for his share in the wars of Kauravas and Pandavas during which, according to all whose opinion possesses any value, the Kshatrya race became extinct and India received a shock from which it has not yet recovered. And yet Rama and Krishna have been honoured, as has been the case with no man, before or after them. The traitors Sugriv and Bhibikhan and the erratic Pandavas, who gambled away their own kingdom, have been immortalized; simply because they were all pro-Brahmans and were of a class that did anything at the bidding of Brahmans. Guru Govind Singh was no advocate of Brahmanical supremacy. His whole life was spent in the service of the weak and the oppressed. Of high descent himself he lived for the people, worked for the people, and died for the people. This explains why no Brahman bard has sung Guru Govind Singh's praise.

Among the world's great men there have been many who have toiled, all through life, in working out an idea. Unmindful of what passed around them great sages have unfurled gates of wisdom. Seekers after scientific knowledge have probed into nature and revealed its mysteries to the wondering humanity. The most renowned of empire-builders and founders of religions have performed their work disregardful of other peoples' feelings and interests. But at all times Guru Govind Singh had a tear for the woe-begone and a smile for the brave spirits struggling to break through the bondage of sin and slavery. His energies were not restricted to one sphere of action and his sympathies were not confined to one class or community. He befriended Mussalmans when they needed his assistance. Amongst his adherents there were not a few who belonged to the Muslim Faith, who were associated with him in his efforts to chastise evil-doers, and who remained steadfast in their loyalty to him till his very last days. Though he inculcated a distinct creed, organised his followers into a distinct community with distinct symbols and distinct ways and beliefs, he was the first and foremost in espousing the cause of the down-trodden Hindus; thus inculcating the principle, which the enlightened Europe learnt centuries later and which the modern Hindus and Hinduized Sikhs, notwithstanding their much vaunted culture, find it difficult to comprehend, that diversity in matters of belief and opinion is no bar to an exchange of courtesies in matters social and political, and that in no way it forbids co-operation in meeting common danger. Indeed, his whole life's work was to chastise those who believed that it was incumbent on them to force every one to their own way of thinking in religious matters and that it was an act of merit, or at least it was no sin to appropriate the belongings of those whose creed was different. If Aurangzebe had adhered to the belief propounded in the Quran that a sovereign is a shadow of God on the Earth and, as such, had treated all his subjects alike, it does not require much effort to imagine that Guru Govind Singh would have confined himself to purely religious work and Musalmans would not have lost their Government.

What a serious mistake some people make when they assign a man of Guru Govind Singh's cosmic sympathy a place among petty politicians and warriors whose best energies were employed in the aggrandisement of their own communities at the sacrifice of other peoples' liberties. True it is that during the latter part of his life the Guru was engaged in a protracted war; but in this war he played only a defensive part. It was not a war of his own seeking. The motive to enrich himself and the community that followed his lead, at the expense of others, did not guide his actions. He took up the cause of the Hindus not because he was connected with them by the tie of blood; but because the atrocious rule to which they were subject had made a hell, as it were, for them, on this earth, to rescue them from which he thought to be his paramount duty. If Hindus had been the oppressors it goes without saying that he would have as boldly and bravely resisted them. Though politically oppressed the high-caste Hindus were most provokingly aggressive in matters religious and social. Guru Govind Singh's whole life was a protest against this aggression. His whole force was employed in exposing the iniquity of the Hindu social system and the major part of his writings consists of most uncompromising criticism of the ways and doings of the Hindu religious hierarchy. Thus it is truly stated in Bachittar Natak, that he had been sent by the Gracious Providence to rescue innocent people from oppression and to chastise evil-doers. In a word, his mission was to elevate the fallen humanity and both by precept and example he showed how this end could be attained.

Before Guru Govind Singh similar efforts have been made in this country. In pre-historic times the erudite Rawan raised the standard of rebellion against the aggressive Brahmans and Kshatryas and perished in the attempt. Mahatma Gautam Budha succeeded in establishing the Kingdom of Righteousness in this country. The rule of the classes gave place to that of the masses. People no longer hated one another. They assembled in public meetings to confer on matters of communal interest. There were Budhist Kings no doubt, but in reality the will of the people was law. This reign of peace and good-will lasted for over a thousand years. But a godless creed, however beneficent in conception, was the last to hold permanent sway over the minds of the Indian people. Rather than have no God the Budhist peasants contrived to install gods of wood and stone in their places of worship. The Brahmans improved upon this. They gave them human gods. The traditional respect which they commanded, their superior intelligence and capacity for organization enabled them, in the course of time, to regain their ascendancy. The seductive teachings of Shankaracharya and other learned reactionaries won over the reigning Rajput families. A concordat was thus arrived at between the two powerful castes, the Brahmans and the Rajputs, into whose hands the government of this country has passed alternately, from time immemorial, to subjugate the mass of the Indian population by means fair or foul. Those who refused to submit to the authority of the coalition were honoured by the names of Asurs, Rakshasas and Yavans and were tortured to death. It is stated that non-conforming Budhists were huddled together into boats and were drowned in the Ganges. Be that as it may in this there can be no doubt that when the sword of Islam, after centuries of employment, failed to exterminate the Hindus, the driving out of millions of the indigenous population into far off uninviting cold countries, or it may be, their extermination, must have been accompanied by horrid forms of torture too difficult to describe.

The hill Rajputs made similar efforts to exterminate the heterodox Sikhs; but though Guru Govind Singh was treacherously vanquished, with the help of the Mughal Emperor, his work left a lasting impress and his assassination and that of his two infant sons created a wave of indignation which spread throughout the land. The Sikhs were converted into a great power as if by magic. They wreaked vengeance on the Muslim tyrants to their hearts' content and before a century elapsed the conservative hierarchy lay prostrate at the feet of the Sikhs. Thus not only the Sikhs were able to hold their own against the overwhelming odds of the enemy, they acquired a position which wrested respect and admiration even from the haughtiest supporters of the Brahmanical supremacy.

Of all vices that have debased humanity, more or less, in all ages and in all countries, selfishness is the most potent one. The greatest enemy of man is man. The statistics of any country may be collected. It will be found that the number of deaths from the attacks of wild animals and poisonous vermin s excluding of course deaths from natural causes, such as disease, old age or other accidents, is infinitesimally small as compared with that due to wars waged to deprive people of their liberty or to murders committed either to take wrongful possession of other peoples' belongings or to encourage acts prompted by lust which is only another form of selfishness. When we closely examine the evolution of human society we find that in all its stages of development it has had among its builders men who had more or less insight into the workings of the human soul and who, with a view to make it as difficult as possible for a person or a set of persons to encroach upon other peoples' rights or to obtain status to which by virtue of their attainments they may not be entitled, have framed laws and to ensure obedience to these laws the authority of both God and man has been requisitioned. But these laws worked satisfactorily only for a short time and so frail is man's nature and so prone is he to err that continued efforts have had to be made at regular intervals to thwart opposition to such authority and rehabilitate it with additional prestige of some sort or other. In individual cases it has been always easy to punish people for their disobedience to such laws; but when men formed mutual defence societies, designated as castes, guilds or so forth, and arrogated to themselves dignities and honours which they were never entitled to, the legislature found it difficult to haul them up before the courts of justice. This is why the All Merciful Providence, from time to time, sends high souled preceptors, like Budha, Christ and Govind Singh, to point out to people the errors of their ways and to tell them how to treat their fellow-men justly. Their contemporaries mostly scoffed at their work; but the history of the human race bears testimony to the good work done by these great benefactors. Wherever the force of their teachings is felt men are comparatively kind and considerate in their dealings with one another.

# CHAPTER XXVI.

Interference with other peoples' beliefs has been and still is the bane of all Asia. It has crippled Asiatic peoples and has impeded their march onwards. Leaving aside one solitary instance of Japan, there is no country in Asia where this feeling of isolation on account of religious opinions is not distinctly pronounced. Even in India, notwithstanding the spread of liberal Western education, men of light and lead in this country are still seen striving after national unity on the bonds of religious affinity. It is sickening to hear, from our pulpits and platforms of a Hindu nation, Sikh nation and a Mussalman nation. Too much stress cannot be laid on pointing out the absurdity of the belief that the members of a religious denomination necessarily form one nationality. Religion, though originally intended to bring people together on a common platform, has never bound together any very large number of men, for a long time. On the contrary, diversity in religious beliefs has been made in all ages and climes the ground for unspeakable barbarities and oppression. European peoples after suffering immensely from outbursts of fanaticism and bigotry have found out the mistake of the heads of their churches and now they are indifferent as to the religious opinions of their countrymen. European nationalities are now based on political rather than on religious interests. And immense has been the gain to humanity for this change. Likewise if the various communities, that inhabit this country, do not realize that they are all descended from one stock, that the blood that runs in their veins is the same, that their destinies are interwoven, and that they must rise together or fall together, no matter what they eat, how they pray, and how they dress, the future of this land is gloomy. Any religious system that does not bind man to man and does not give birth to feelings of amity and accord is as good as useless.

In these days of political clap-trap when glib-tongued haranguers have monopolized the pulpit and the platform, when the excitement of race-hatred and fanaticism are synonyms for patriotism and public service it will be refreshing to read the following extract from the Lahore *Tribune* in which the writers attempt a forecast of the nationalization of the Indian races.

"I wish to emphasize the opinion of a correspondent in a recent issue of your paper who speaks with so much feeling of the gradual nationalization of the Indian races, the 'welding together of all the races and castes in India into a national whole.' We must all understand, once for all, as to what is involved in this noble aspiration, and then work our way steadfastly to the goal, turning neither to the right nor to the left. Let me say, at once, that to my mind, the 'Indian Nation' of the future will be neither an exclusively Hindu nor Muhammadan nor Christian nation; but, though based largely upon the noblest traditions and traits of character of its largest component, it will include all these three as well as the lesser communities. Doubtless, as your correspondent points out, there are several forces at work which tend ultimately to unite the whole peninsula "in one single fraternal bond;" but we must not shut our eyes to the fact that, at the same time, there are forces, apparently feeble yet capable of being readily fanned to a fury, which make for disruption. Now if we would be a nation, it is our duty to strengthen the forces of union against those of disruption, and this we can best do by social intercourse and the practice of charity and religious toleration. It is this spirit which has made Japan a great nation. In the absence of this cardinal virtue it will be vain for us to look for an Indian nation. Togo, the great Japanese Admiral, as well as the victor of the battle of Chemulphu, are Christians. In Japan it is not an uncommon thing for a Shinto father and a Christian son to live under the same roof. It will, perhaps, be a long time before we reach the same stage in India; but we see that, even in an Asiatic country, the purest and highest patriotism can dwell in the midst of religious differences. Why should it be otherwise in India?"*

The same paper has the following extracts from the *Hindu*, a Madras daily, and from the reply of the Maharaja Adhiraj of Burdwan, to the address presented by the Burdwan Muhammadan Association, in its issues of July 11th, 1908, and February 1st, 1909, A. D. They are given here to show that correct ideas are gaining hold throughout the length and the breadth of the land.

"The time has come without doubt in the history of modern India, when its people should not need the services of special missionaries to straighten their

* *Tribune, dated June 11th*, 1904.

social system and when the progress of society should be accelerated by the assimilation of progressive ideas in the mass of the people, and by the community advancing as a whole, independent of extraneous propelling influences. It is, we think, a blot on the capacity of the Indian people for progressive adaptation to circumstances that their progress in social matters has been slow. What is the cause of this? In writing about the nations of the East, J. S. Mill says: "Those nations must once have had originality. They did not start out of the ground populous, lettered and versed, in many of the arts of life. They made themselves all this and were then the greatest and most powerful nations in the world. What are they now? The subjects or dependents of tribes whose forefathers wandered in the forests when theirs had magnificent palaces and gorgeous temples; but over whom custom exercised only a divided rule with liberty and progress. A people, it appears, may be progressive for a certain length of time, and then stop. When does it stop? When it ceases to possess individuality." It is pointed out that in the East, 'the despotism of custom is complete—custom is there in all things the final appeal.' This is, indeed, the cause of the all social stagnation which is to be observed in this country; and until the dominion of custom which is stereotyped in some of the social institutions of the country is broken down and free scope is given to individuality, no great progress, in the direction in which national life should grow, is possible. We have recently come across the case of an English Missionary gentleman who is the head of an educational institution in this Presidency, who is an exceptionally kind-hearted teacher, and shows himself absorbed in the welfare and improvement of his pupils. It is his practice to take out his pupils on excursions into the villages for the purpose of nature-instruction and for relaxation; and the difficulties he has had to encounter for food, when in company with his high caste pupils, were narrated in such a manner as to make his Hindu auditor blush for the customs and social habits of his countrymen."

"It has been a laid down policy in this Raj to show a spirit of tolerance to every creed and cult, and to the Muhammadans particularly; for the Burdwan Raj owes its existence to the Moghul Emperors, and you may be certain that fully aware as I am of my responsibilities, this policy will never be lost sight of by me. Further, I look upon you, Muhammadans, just as much my brother countrymen as my brother-Hindus. You are a potent factor in the national life of India. Without you that unit which alone could build up India as a nation could never come into existence. It pains me whenever I come across any incident relating to friction between Hindus and Muhammadans; for you may be the followers of Islam, and we may be the followers of the Vedas; but we are Indians. India to you is just as much the mother country as it is to us. Her interests should be as much the interests of the Muhammadans as of the Hindus, and I, therefore, hope that you will always remember this fact, and that in this district, we Hindus and Muhammadans may always live in harmony as we have done in the past, and go on working for the good of our country, standing shoulder to shoulder, in calamities as well as during periods of exultation and joy."

No people are God's chosen ones. He helps those who act up to His principles. So far and so long as a people act up to these principles they are able to do good to themselves and to others. If instead of these life-giving principles they are guided in their actions by sordid motives they lose the sustaining moral force and become politically extinct, sooner or later.

"God first created light", says Bhagat Kabir. "All are subordinate to the inexorable nature. The whole world is an emanation from the same One Light. Whom shall we call good and whom bad? The Creator is in the creation and creation is in the Creator. His spirit permeates all."

The famous Punjabi Muslim saint, Bulleh Shah, sings in the same strain:—

Sahiyo merí bukal vich chor.
Koí Rám Dás, koí Fateh Mohammad eh hai qadímí shor.

"Friends, the thief is within me. Some I regard as Ram Dass's; some Fateh Mohammads. This is the old old strife."

Guru Govind Singh thus proclaims the Fatherhood of God and the brotherhood of man:—

Jaise ek ág te kanúká kot ág uthe niyáre niyáré hoe kai phir ág men miláhenge;
Jaise ek dhúr te anek dhúr púrat hai dhúr ke kanúká pher dhúr hí samáenge;

Jaise ek nád te tarang kot upj hai pán ke tarang
sabai pán hi kahaenge.

Taise biswa rúp te abhút bhút pragat hoe táhin
te upj sabai táhin men samáenge.

"As from one fire numberless sparks of fire rise and part and again join in fire;

as from a cloud of dust numberless dust clouds spread over the sky and particles of dust again lose themselves in dust;

as from one river numberless waves rise up and waves of water will always be called water;

similarly from the Being of whom the Universe is a manifestation forms of spirit and matter appearing will lose themselves from where they came."

Verily, it is man's vicious self that prompts him to look down on his fellow beings merely on account of difference of opinion in matters of belief. Some religions may be more cosmic in their ministration of beneficence, others less so; but religious systems which permit man-hatred are baneful in the extreme.

Guru Govind Singh's religion was a religion of love to man and devotion to God. All his life he laboured to see to the harmonious development of his country. As has been previously stated if he took up arms it was not to acquire a kingdom for himself or to deprive other people of their liberty. He opposed the Rajput Rajas of the northern Punjab when they provoked him, and he resisted the Moghul power when it sought to crush him altogether and when it interfered with his mission of establishing the reign of good-will and peace. In this respect, Guru Govind Singh stands alone among the world's great benefactors and in this lies the peculiarity of his mission. He was a patriot; but his patriotism was of a higher type, of not an aggressive kind. He was an angel sent down to minister to the needy, to protect the defenceless and to raise the lowly. The merest dregs of society, even sweepers, whose very touch was pollution, were purified and allotted positions side by side with high-caste Brahmans and Kshatriyas from among the disciples. The rich and the great vied with one another in parting with their wealth, in order that the poor among them might be above want; and the poor, in their turn, rendered willing service and made themselves useful so that they might not be looked down by their superiors. The whole tone of the community was highly moral. The thoughts of the believers were pure and their lives temperate. They lived not for lucre or for fame. The smiles of royalty and the bestowal of *Jagirs* had no charm for them. Life itself was not regarded by them as worth anything if it was not spent in the service of the *Panth*, or if it necessitated renunciation of the Guru or of the *Panth*. "Many stories are told!" says Khafi Khan, the historian of the times of Aurangzebe and a few later Moghul Emperors, "about the dogs of this sect which the understanding rejects; but the author will relate what he saw with his own eyes. When the executions were going on, the mother of one of the prisoners, a young man just arrived at manhood, having obtained some influential support, pleaded the cause of her son, with great feeling and earnestness, before the Emperor and Syad Abdullah Khan. She represented that her son had suffered imprisonment and hardship at the hands of the sect. His property was plundered and he was made prisoner. While in captivity, he was, without any fault of his own, introduced into the sect and now stood innocent among those sentenced to death. Farukh Siyar commisserated this artful woman, and mercifully sent an officer with orders to release the youth. That cunning woman arrived with the order of release just as the executioner was standing with his bloody sword upheld over the young man's head. She showed the order for his release. The youth, then, broke out into complaints saying "my mother tells a falsehood. I, with my heart and soul, join my fellow-believers in my devotion to the Guru. Send me quickly after my companions."*

To a community consisting of men with such brave souls and united by ties so noble, the Guru left his own *Guddee* and invested them with power to govern in matters spiritual and temporal. A council of elders, consisting of all classes of people, was formed. Matters of moment were submitted to it and its decisions were respectfully obeyed. This unique commonwealth, based not on the principles of Liberty, Fraternity and Equality; but on that of sacrifice for common good, for which purpose considerations of self had, of course, to be set aside, was established in an Asiatic country, under the sway of one of the most unscrupulous and tyrannical of despots

* [Sir Charles Elliot—History of India, as told by its own historians].

that have ever disgraced a throne; and though this commonwealth ceased to exist, upwards of a century later, for want of intelligent, far-seeing and unselfish leaders, the success that it achieved, during its short existence, will serve as an object-lesson to every Indian patriot of whatever race or creed and will cheer him up in the most dismal of moments.

# CHAPTER XXVII.

Modern Sikhs are generally not good specimens of what true Sikhs were only half a century back. They are not inspired with any marked degree of zeal for the propagation of their creed. Places of worship are visited and scriptures read as a mere matter of form. At none of the principal *Gurudwaras* the cardinal doctrines of the Sikh belief are daily instilled into the minds of the believers, as was the case in the time of the Gurus. In fact there is a dearth of *Gyanis* or interpreters of the scriptures. The *Nirmalas*, a sect of Sikh *Sadhus*, founded by the 10th Guru, who are well up both in the Sikh and Sanskrit lore and count among them thinkers and debaters, who would be an acquisition to any community, have mostly gone over to Hinduism, and it is they who are mostly responsible for the Hinduising of the Sikh creed. To an orthodox Sikh outward forms are mostly more important than inward purity. To him an ideal Sikh is a veritable coxcomb who can conveniently wear all popular forms of Sikhism, and can babble out, parrot-like, a few passages from the scriptures. This disregard of inward culture is, to no small extent, responsible for the mental prostration of the mass of the community; and it is on account of this alone that so many imposters, whether of old or new type, find it so easy to get a following, from the mass of the Sikh population. In place of the Brahman priesthood, a comparatively less intellectual, but not less perverse, priesthood has acquired a thorough mastery over the Sikh mind. The *Sahjdhari* Sikhs are seceding and going over to the communities who do not assign to them an inferior rank among them. The 10th Guru did not insist that all his followers should receive *Amrita.* There were many who did not take *Amrita*; but remained faithful to him. Only those were baptised to the Faith and wore the symbols, *Kará* (an iron bracelet), *Kachha* (short drawers), *Kirpán* (dagger), *Keshas* (uncut head hair) and *Kangha* (comb), who took a vow of renunciation and offered themselves to be sacrificed in the service of the *Panth.* In a word the baptismal ceremony was voluntary. It was not forced upon any one. Only heroes and martyrs received the distinction of baptism. But no discrimination is now exercised in the performance of the ceremony. The form and the symbols remain; but the spirit seems to have mostly flown away. Take off the sacred thread of a Hindu, take off his *Bodi* (hair tuft on the head) he is a Hindu. A Christian may eat any thing, may dress any way, he does not cease to be a Christian. But take away the symbols of a Sikh and he is lost to the community!

Sikhism has come to this pass that its well-wishers have felt prompted to recommend that it should pray for a longer lease of life from a Government professing a different religion. The *Times of India*, an Anglo-Indian journal of Bombay, thus wrote in one of its issues in 1903 A. D.:—

"An anonymous writer in the *Empire Review* has discovered a novel duty for the Government of India. It is that they should accord official recognition and support to the religion of the Sikhs. The Sikhs, argues the writer, make the best Indian soldiers and it is their religion that makes them so. A decline of Sikhism, therefore, would mean a decline of the military strength of the Empire. The State is consequently interested in the maintenance of that Faith and without State recognition and support the decline cannot be checked. Writings such as the article under notice are mischievous. From the support of a religion, for political reasons, to the propagation of it, for the same reasons, is but a narrow step. There would be reason for anxiety about the precarious position in the modern world of State neutrality in matters of belief, if there were any considerable number of thoughtful men favouring the view which finds expression in the *Empire Review*. But it is not so; and effusions such as those under notice should be regarded as instances of intellectual atavism—the reappearance after an interval of generations of an obsolete idea, in a modern writer." The *Civil and Military Gazette*, the Lahore Anglo-Indian daily, in its issue of April 15th, 1903, thus expressed itself on modern Sikhism, in the course of a leading article:—

"Sikhism appears a remarkable creed. It organized the Hindu Jat cultivators of the Punjab, who had been content to submit to each successive horde of invaders and pay taxes to Tartar and Pathan, Mughal and Pathan again, with no more serious resistance than an occasional outbreak of dacoity, into a formidable military power, more closely united than the Marhattas and held together by religious fervour as well as by the instinct of national resistance to the foreign Muhammadan power. It is not a little remarkable that a faith so simple in its dogmas and so alien to the spirit of older Hindu religions, should have been able to effect so complete a change in the character of its votaries, metamorphosing even the outcaste and despised "Chuhra" into the Mazahbi, a very respectable fighting man, as the records of our Pioneer regiments abundantly testify. The present position of Sikhism is, however, very unsatisfactory. It is not one of the proselytizing religions and barely holds its own. No doubt among the Jats of the Punjab proper, its vitality is unimpaired; but while it preaches equality it fails to give full practical effect to its leading doctrines; and in the Sikh districts the low-castes turn not to Sikhism but to Christianity. To the student of Indian religions Sikhism appears doomed to share the fate of Budhism and the religion of the Jains—of every one of the great social and religious movements which have arisen in India and endeavoured to shake off the bonds of the tyranny of the caste system and the spiritual despotism of Brahmanical Hinduism. Certain races, at a given stage of their development, appear incapable of supporting the bracing atmosphere of constitutional government or rational religions and resign themselves to a military despotism and a dominant priesthood and the Indian races have always been so ruled, in the mass; though from time to time there have arisen movements to protest against the system. The present position of Sikhism, as a social force is, we think, also unsatisfactory. It is in danger of losing its great distinctive features and merging into the dead level of its surroundings; and, perhaps, in a generation or two, it will only survive like the Cameronians in the title of a few historic regiments."

The above extract from the *Civil and Military Gazette* will be read by all Sikhs with a grateful feeling; for evidently the writer thereof seems to have been actuated by a desire to see Sikhism occupy a respectable place among the religions of the world. But it should not be forgotten that, however high and ennobling a system of beliefs may be, it must take time to completely influence the lives of a community. Guru Govind Singh's life was spent among Rajputs and Khatris whom conceit and prejudice of ages had completely blinded and who, just as the Jews saw no beauty in Christ's Gospel, were either indifferent or opposed to the Guru's mission. The Barar clan of the Malwa Jats who followed the Guru's lead though brave, generous, guileless and confiding, were least intellectual at the time; and just as the fanatic Mussalmans of Central Africa are the last people on the face of the Earth to understand the higher aspects of Islam, the Jat population of the Punjab, who had never come in contact with enlightenment, were not capable of continually spreading the Guru's propaganda in its entirety. To them to be Sikh was to avow open hatred for Brahmans and Mussalmans. Men, with a strong arm, ready to strike a blow on the Mussalmans and fit to suffer great physical hardships were principally in demand and when these people succeeded in crushing the Muslim power they only demanded adherance to outward symbols of Sikhism. Mussalmans subdued, the discreet high-caste Hindus made advances for a conciliation with the new power. A compromise was effected by which the Sikhs abandoned their revolutionary programme and the Hindus included the names of the ten Gurus among the incarnations of Vishnu. From that time Sikhism may be said to have commenced losing its distinct individuality and the Lahore *Tribune* was right when, commenting on the agitation started in the above-mentioned Anglo-Indian journals, it observed in its issue of May 7th, 1903, that "the greater the room and scope of military service the greater will be the numerical strength and prosperity of the Khalsa. No apprehension need be felt as to the supply of Sikh soldiers ever falling short of the demand. The boy in the family, among the stalwart Hindu rustics in the Punjab, who is destined for a career of arms, is given the suffix "Singh" to his name, wears long hair and becomes a Khalsa. So, as long as recruiting officers will prefer Sikh lads, Sikh lads will be forthcoming."

The remarks of the writer in the *Tribune* are no doubt true to a large extent. This predominance of mercenary feelings in the *Panth* is a matter for serious concern. Evidently the keeping of uncut hair has ceased to necessarily indicate a belief in the teachings of the 10th Guru. The men who enlist in the army and take 'Pahul' do mostly for lucre and, if this object can be secured without keeping long hair, long hair will not adorn their heads. The situation is serious enough to demand the earnest attention of the thinking portion of the community. At present there is no guarantee that the men who seek admission into the *Panth* do so from worldly motives or otherwise. Strict adherance to the Guru's principles should be insisted upon so that it may become difficult or not worth while for men to leave the Sikh fold after they have once entered it.

As previously stated Government support has neither been sought nor offered. But Government officers have not been altogether unmindful of Sikh interests. They have always a good word to say for the Sikhs and thus keep up their ideas of self-respect and courage. The last brilliant Viceroy, Lord Curzon, when presented with an address by tho Khalsa Diwan of Lahore, on April 5th, 1899, during the days when the Lahore Sikhs were making rejoicings, on the occasion of the 2nd centenary of the foundation of the Khalsa Panth, thus alluded to the Sikhs :—"Your Honour and Gentlemen. In responding to the address which was presented to me, a few days ago, by the Municipality of Lahore, I spoke of the Punjab as the home of a race that produces not merely men but heroes. When I used that phrase I did not know that I should have the pleasure, before I left this city, of meeting a representative body of the nationality to whom it obviously applied. The incident of Saragarhi, to which you refer in your address, is one of several that were in my mind in making the remark in question. There are many qualities required to constitute the ideal soldier, bravery, endurance, a certain aptitude of intellect and discipline; but I am not sure that above them all I would not place that unfaltering devotion to duty and heroic disregard of self that impels a man to die at his post, as the Sikhs at Saragarhi did, unmurmuring and even happy, fighting against overwhelming odds. Of this virtue the Sikh soldiers of the army of the Queen have given many an illustration, in fifty years of fighting for the British Raj, since the time, when they fought so well against us; so that the name of your race has become almost synonymous, in the English language, with traditions of desperate courage and unflinching loyalty.......Never may the day arrive when the British Government, in time of need, can not rely upon his (Sikh soldier's) staunch and unquestioning service.......Nevertheless in the modern world, military virtues, however pre-eminent, are not the only requisites to the preservation of national existence and you have wisely realized that, if you are to hold your own with the more erudite peoples, among whom you are placed, you must provide your families with an education compatible with theirs. I am pleased to learn that the Khalsa College has already attained to a high standard of excellence and I hope that it may continue to receive the active support of the Sikh princes of the Punjab and may turn out a number of young men who, like Lord Lawrence, in the famous statue which stands in this city, may be competent to wield the pen at the same time that their other hand rests confidently upon the hilt of the sword."*

Only recently Sir Charles Rivaz, the then Lieutenant-Governor of the Punjab, spent six days in Amritsar. Representative Sikhs from all India assembled and nearly twenty lacs of rupees were

* Quoted from the *Khalsa* of April 12th, 1899.

subscribed in aid of the College. In addition to this the district officers in Sikh districts threw themselves into the work of collecting funds for the Khalsa College with an enthusiasm that wrested admiration from all Sikhs and caused not a little heart-burning in non-Sikh circles. Thus, in a manner, the civil power has lent the weight of its influence in favour of the Sikhs. Opinions, however, differ as to the ultimate result of such extraneous help.

All European writers, however, do not take a very desponding view of the situation. "Notwithstanding these changes," says Cunningham, in his History of the Sikhs, * "it has been usual to regard the Sikhs as essentially Hindu and they doubtless are so in their language and every-day customs; for Govind Singh did not fetter his disciples with political systems or codes of Municipal laws; yet in religious faith and worldly aspirations they are wholly different from other Indians; and they are bound together by a community of inward sentiment and of outward object unknown elsewhere. But the misapprehension need not surprise the public nor our scholars, when it is remembered that the learned of Greece and Rome misunderstood the spirit of those humble men who obtained a new life by baptism. Tacitus and Suetonius regarded the Christians as a mere Jewish sect. They failed to perceive the fundamental difference and to appreciate the latent energy and real excellence of that doctrine which has added dignity and purity to modern civilization."

* [Edition of 1849, A. D.)

This is exactly the view we take of the mission of our creed. We do not believe that the seed sown by the Gurus and fed by the blood of thousands of our martyrs is dead.

With all their faults the Sikhs, properly so called, are brave and generous as compared with their other fellow-countrymen. Though they do not follow in its entirety the programme of their great leaders they are socially and religiously on a higher plane and their Hindu compatriots have been very largely influenced by them in matters social and religious. Hindus, in the Punjab, are very liberal in their thoughts and deeds as compared with their co-religionists in other parts of India. They all freely inter-dine. Such a thing as separate *chawkas* (dining rooms) for members of the same families is not known in the Punjab. No one is excommunicated for crossing the seas. The question never arises to which caste the cooks should belong. In places where the influence of the Sikhs is most felt it is the practice to employ Muhammadans to fetch water. Imbibing this spirit hordes of Punjabi Hindus emigrate to Balkh, Bukhara and Yarqand, the chief centres of Mussalman commerce and industry, and acquire riches and affluence. Though yet not quite free from the clutches of the Brahmans they do not view the remarriage of widows with disfavour. The feeling is general and real that enforced widowhood is a crying evil and crime against society and it does not require a prophet to foretell that many years will not elapse before the Punjabis will proclaim a rebellion against this social tyranny. The remarriage of widows is already an institution among the Sikh Jats who form the most pre-eminent part of the Sikh community. Similarly in other matters of reform the Punjabi Hindus are remarkably bold and forward. All this is due to Guru Govind Singh's teaching which infuses chivalry into all who come under its influence.

# CHAPTER XXVIII.

The safety of the Sikhs lies in their keeping the integrity of their creed intact. If they cease to lose their individuality they will cease to exist in a few generations more. Their Gurus were honoured, in their time, because they were the noblest of their contemporaries and when they waged war against superstition, sin and slavery, no other force was operating for the good of the country. The state of things is now changed. The work of reform has now been taken up by the enlightened men of all sections of the Indian community. The anti-Muslim and anti-Brahman propaganda with which the Sikh pioneers started work has lost its force; for neither the Muslims nor the Brahmans are now in a position to tyrannize over anybody, thanks to Pax Brittanica. In order that Sikhism should be able to attract modern humanity it should be in a position to offer something more conducive to the well-being of mankind than what the votaries of other creeds are prepared to give. The Muslim tyrants have been brought to the knee. The Brahmans, in this country, have practically lost their supremacy. But the political work done by the Sikhs is only a closed chapter in the history of their country. The Sikh Church requires reconstruction. The Guru's ideal of spreading the Sikh creed, of raising the saints and rooting out all evildoers,* of founding the Kingdom of Righteousness

---

* Dharm chaláwan sant ubáran.
Dusht sabhan ko múl upáran.

on this Earth, of bringing all men on the platform of equality, of inter-dependence, of acquiring communal might and affluence* is an ever present duty to perform which unceasing, whole hearted efforts are needed.

"It is difficult," says Smiles, in his book, Character, "to swim against the stream but every dead fish can float along with it." Men who cannot think for themselves, who look up to this or that person to tell them that this is right and that is wrong, whom custom and tradition alone guide, are like the dead fish. All their life they keep floating along with the current of popular opinion. It is not such men who form the vital force of a social organism. The greater the number of such men in a community the more weak it is. Such men are a danger to the State. They readily fall into snare. Ambitious and designing individuals appeal to their deep-rooted prejudices and fanaticism and employ them as tools.

The ambitious platform orator dilates on the superiority of this person or that class. He does not look to harmonious communal development. He waxes eloquent over the great achievements of our common Aryan forefathers. He publishes to the world that our progenitors were noble and enlightened when the ancestors of the Western peoples roamed in jungles. He flatters our pride; but accounts not for our fall. He proclaims with a flourish that the ancient Egyptians and Saracens,

* "Deg teg fateh."

Romans and Greeks have all died; but he does not explain what pride there is in an inert existence. If one follows him, panders to the passions of the populace, he is an ornament of the community. If he takes one real, bold step, in reform, breaks off from the thraldom of custom, he is nowhere. Down comes on him the wrath of the thundering pulpit haranguer. His subsidised newspapers discharge salvos of invective. His paid emissaries scatter the poison and the go-ahead man stands practically ostracized.

This cheap patriotism has thrown the work of real reform centuries backwards. Castes and races previously divided people. Denominational institutions, born of race hatred and bred on fanaticism, have torn them asunder still further. This wave of fanaticism has carried all before it. The Sikh Dispensation, conceived and nurtured by saints and hallowed by the blood of martyrs, ought to make no distinction in its ministration of beneficence. Not unlike a conscientious physician who makes no distinction of race, creed or colour, it should ungrudgingly apply balm on all soring hearts who may come to it for cure. Nay, with the bowl of "Amrita" in hand it should knock at every door and tell all who are disconsolate that they can yet be happy, that they can yet rise and live joyous lives if they take a sip from the Nectar and take the "Vow of Renunciation," the vow to love and minister to the wants of their fellowmen without distinction; for God makes no distinction, the Gurus made no distinction.

But if it is absurd to put new wines into old bottles, if it is absurd to turn back the dial of time, it is equally absurd to start anew in all respects and to ignore the experience of our great Aryan ancestors. We have our own scriptures no doubt; but, equally with other races of Aryan extraction, we ought to feel a natural pride in the achievements of our progenitors and should consider it a bounden duty to preserve all that may be worth preserving. No one has done more to popularise Bhakti (devoutness), piety and several other elevating phases of the religion preached in the Puranas than the Sikh Gurus and the later Sikh writers. Indeed it is no exaggeration to say that the mass of the Punjab Hindus receive spiritual ministration through Sikh Sadhus and Sikh Scriptures.

It cannot be said with certainty what the future of Sikhism will be. Any such forecast must necessarily be based on conjecture. But examined from all points of view the Sikhism of Guru Govind Singh presents features which all tend to create the impression that it has not yet played out its part. It is only passing through a stage of transition and, just as the light of the Christian Faith shone dimly during the Dark Ages and men's minds remained comparatively un-illumined, the inculcation of the heart-consoling principles of Sikhism has been, so to speak, kept in abeyance, amid the warring passions of the combatants that have been fighting for political supremacy, in this country, during the last century and a half. But now that peace has been restored and western knowledge has been diffused, far and wide, the Sikhs, along with other communities, have been awakened to a sense of their responsibility and though the efforts of the workers among them are yet feeble and their results are consequently not remarkable, it may be confidently predicted that, with a number of earnest and sincere workers of good morale, Sikhism may yet live to be a leading creed. All that is wanted is to arrange for the propagation of the Sikh Gospel and insist upon the practical observance of its unalloyed principles, without regard to what other people think or say.

Guru Govind Singh's life and teachings possess an eternal charm. His writings possess a force that will, for all time, infuse spirit even into the merest poltroon and will raise dead men into life, as it were. His is the highest example of piety, fellow-feeling and sacrifice. If people make him their ideal and learn to walk in his footsteps they will become self-reliant and self-repecting. Their faith in the Timeless One will help them in rating what the world can give at its proper value. Wealth and splendour will cease to tempt them and the smiles or the frowns of the world's despots will fail to seduce them. Their word will become law, their look command. No savage hand shall molest them. No evil heart shall dare disturb the peace of their hearths and homes. The Western Materialism, which has created artificial wants, and has filled people with an inordinate passion for riches, which takes not much into account how its votaries come by wealth and power, which has failed to solve the population and poverty problems, will once again bow before our Eastern Spiritualism which forbids indulgence in any form, which regards this life only as a period of apprenticeship for a higher and nobler existence and which regards it a sin that one brother should roll in wealth while the other groans in poverty. "First" say our Scriptures "vow to die. Give up hope of life. Become the dust of every one's feet. Then come to me."*

---

* Pahle maran qabúl, jíwan dí chhad ás ;
Ho sagal kí ren-ká tau áo hamáre pás.

# CHAPTER XXIX.

I have omitted all mention of the miracles attributed to the Guru. A Sikh contractor to whom I mentioned this fact strongly disapproved of my action. He believed, and there may be many who agree with him, that in so doing I have placed the subject of this memoir in the lower rank of the founders of other great creeds. I do not, however, plead guilty to the accusation. I do not believe that such miracles were ever performed. They mostly signify efforts to prevent the working of the laws of nature and the men who base the greatness of their heroes on the extent to which they could suspend the operation of these laws do not explain why the great men at whose caprice the elements changed the functions assigned to them by the Great Maker of the Universe had to submit, one and all, to the great irrevocable law that all who are born must die. According to the Guru "What the Lord graciously giveth is a miracle"* than which a clearer exposition is impossible to give. Nothing can be more astonishing than the boundless love of the Merciful Providence which takes not into account our many an act of omission and commission and rears and protects us from birth to death. To my mind the greatness of the world's great epoch makers lay not in their freaks and caprice; but in their capacity to comprehend God's laws and in their ability to make their followers act in conformity with these

---

* Sahib tuthe jo mile Nának sá karámát.

laws. Judged in this light the mission of Guru Govind Singh has been a unique success. It is more than raising the dead when his boast that he would make hawks of sparrows was realized, when he infused life into the hitherto inert mass of humanity that inhabited the Punjab, when each individual who wore his uniform really believed and showed that he embodied the strength and vigour of a lac and quarter of men. And it is a true prophecy that he made when he said that the sandy wastes of the South-Eastern Punjab would be converted into smiling fields of wheat which they now are—really a marvel of Sikh industry.

On the contrary I hold that Guru Govind Singh openly discarded the theory of miracles. If he had any faith in it he would not have characterized miraculous performances of the deified heroes of Indian mythology as 'Parpanch,' (trickeries.) How could he, then, consistently perform deeds which he ridiculed when done by others? The greatness of Guru Govind Singh, it may be repeated, lay in his elevating millions of men who were hitherto content to be used as chattel and beasts of burden by the high-caste and high-placed men of their own country and the members of the ruling race, in making them self-respecting and self-reliant, in endowing them with iron-will and unbending resolution, and in creating in them a capacity to rule themselves and others. To him steel was a symbol of power. He remembered God generally as All-Steel and attributed his success to the grace of All-Steel. With All-Steel as his model he strove to make his men strong as steel. So long as his followers retained this strength of character their star was in ascendancy; but when they lost sight of the ideal chalked out for them by their great leader, when they failed to act upon the principles of life laid down by him, when they yielded to their grosser self and ignored and sacrificed communal interests, they fell and gave place to a people higher in character and more capable of assuming and discharging public responsibilities.

How truly it has been said that history repeats itself. When the sturdy peasants of Rome, who had not yet come under the enervating influences of ill-gotten wealth and power, met, deliberated and made laws for communal good, and obeyed these laws, they were feared and respected. Their achievements in Politics, Law and Social Autonomy, which have won for them eternal fame, all relate to this period. But when they became unscrupulous and greedy, when all their energy was spent in enslaving their fellow-men, when they subdued great nations of antiquity and carved out for themselves one of the greatest Empires the world has ever seen, when the spoil of distant lands swelled their fortunes, when princes and princesses of foreign lands were made captives and served as pages and household altendants of the Roman nobility and gentry, when their places of residence and public resort were built of marble and were bedecked in precious stones and inlaid in gold, when all that wealth and power could procure adorned their tables and filled their cellars, in a word, when they mistakenly believed that they were a mighty and great people, when men of letters employed themselves in singing their country's glory, the State was rotten in reality, its spirit had flown away and its body alone had remained. No wonder, then, that the barbarians from the north, nay their women, unarmed and stooping under the, weight of the infants they carried on their backs, should have made footballs of the stately Romans, and should have easily over-run the whole Empire and made themselves its masters.

The same is the case with the Greeks. When they subordinated their individual interests to those of the State, when mothers laid the first stone to bury alive their own sons, guilty of treachery to their fatherland, when a handful of men kept hordes of Persian invaders at bay, when such a thing as state-craft was unknown, when men, though blunt and bluff, understood and acted upon the simple principles of polity, they won a position for themselves among the great nations of the world. But no sooner they bade adieu to these principles, and envy, jealousy, and lust for power took hold of their minds, they fell to rise no more. The subtle philosophy which the few inculcated fewer still understood. The master word-painters harangued the people in vain. Their rhetoric, wanting as it did in sincerity of conviction, failed in its effect. Both the leaders and the led strayed from the path of rectitude. The whole State was morally prostrated and fell an easy prey into the hands of the great Alexander.

The same is the story of the rise and fall of all the great nations of the world. When the Sikhs were infinitesimally small, as compared with their present number, when they were hunted, like wild beasts by the Government of the day, when prizes were set on their heads, when renegades from amongst themselves and their Hindu brethren lived upon such rewards, when they hid themselves in far off wildernesses, when the caves and dens in which they found shelter were set fire to by their pursuers and thus proved graves for most of them, when their food was coarse and their garments rude, rather, when they subsisted on the leaves and barks of trees and covered their nakedness with skins, they were a terror to their unscrupulous persecutors. They had no commissariat, no transport, no reserve militia and no treasury. But when they rallied forth from their fastnesses, they were sure of victory. Their number was small, but their hearts were united. They had all one aim and one ambition—to overthrow tyrannic rule. The thought of self never entered their minds. Lust, avarice, and luxury, were unknown to them. They regarded life as transient and all its enjoyments sinful. Such a people were sure of success in any work they took upon themselves. They succeeded in throwing off the yoke of the Muslims who, though rich and powerful, were not so well organized and so well brought up. But when the Sikhs transplanted the Muslims in the government of the country, when the changed surroundings left little scope for the exercise of the virtues that had made them brave and manly, when luxury found admittance into their homes, when, not unlike their predecessors in government, they indulged in unbridled licence, when principles of administration laid down by Guru Govind Singh were ignored, when the Sikh Commonwealth passed into the hands of an individual or individuals and thus no opportunities were left for the cultivation of communal feelings and the discharge of communal responsibilities and, finally, when mercenary instincts governed the actions of the Sikhs, the State passed into other hands.

This is what we learn from history. These are the miracles which the great Divine Maker performs, from time to time, to show how frail are the jackals of tyranny, everywhere, though armed with the most horrid of weapons of torture and death which human ingenuity can invent, to invite attention to the much neglected, but, all the same, inexorable law, that "Righteousness alone exalteth a nation."

# CHAPTER XXX.

It will not be out of place to compare Guru Govind Singh's work with his nine predecessors in the "Guddee." Baba Nanak, the founder of the Sikh creed, was a contemporary of John Knox, Calvin and Luther, and not unlike them he devoted the best part of a long life in pointing out the absurdity of depending for salvation on ritualism in which both Hindus and Mussalmans mostly believed. He called upon men to rely solely on the protection of the Lord who was always with them and whom they could easily please by right thinking and right living. He remembered God as if He was his husband and himself as His spouse and thought it unchaste to give a place to any other person or object in his heart. From Balkh, Bukhara and Khorasan, on one side, to Assam on the other, and from the lakes of Mansrovar and Kuenlin mountains to Ceylon, accompanied by his family bard Mardana, he sang the song of his Beloved's glory, with the accompaniment of the harp. Men inflated with the pride of caste and vitiated by the lust of power sneered at him and sometimes, even, refused him the shelter of their roofs. They ridiculed the novel idea propounded by him that all men were equal in the sight of the Lord and to show the antipathy with which they received his doctrine they called him *Kuráhi* (heretic). But the woe-begone and the lowly heard him with rapture and found consolation in his company. When he appeared darkness was dispelled and the world was illumined.*

* Sat Gur Nanak pragatiyá mití dhund jag chánan hoá.

The places his feet touched became seats of worship.† A brotherhood was thus formed and it was found necessary that the Baba should have some one to whom he could bequeathe his life's work, when death would take him away from the scene of his labours. Such a successor he found in Bhai Lehna, a disciple whom for his devotion to himself and to his cause he named Angad, part and parcel of his own body, and who, as also Guru Amar Das, the 3rd in succession, faithfully followed in his wake and consolidated the Church established by him. The 4th Guru, Ram Das, in addition to spiritual ministration, distinguished himself in acts of benevolence and charity and the famous Golden Temple at Amritsar was constructed in his honour by his son, Guru Arjan. The foundation stone of the temple was laid by Hazrat Mian Mir, the premier Muslim saint of the time. Guru Arjan compiled *Granth Sahib*, the Sikh Scriptures, in which, in addition to his own compositions, he included not only the writings of his four predecessors in the "Guddee"; but those of Hindu and Mussalman saints also, setting the first example in the history of religions, in equally honouring godly men, professing other creeds—an example which all true Sikhs consider it a privilege to follow. Guru Har Govind was the first Guru who felt the necessity of infusing military spirit into his people, took an active part in the Politics of the period and fought several battles with the Mughal Government in which he mostly vanquished his opponents. Guru Tegh Bahadar also

---

† Jithai Baba pair dharai pújá ásan thápan soá.
Vár I of Bhai Gurdas.

followed in his father's wake and won the name he bore by many an act of bravery. Guru Govind Singh gave the finishing touch to the Dispensation brought by his predecessors in the "Guddee". He called for the active display of heart virtues in the service of humanity. The call met with a hearty response. Men learnt to resist tyranny and oppression. The hitherto down-trodden and spiritless Hindus presented a bold front. The ruthless Pathan, the crafty Mughal and the parasitical Brahman, looked bewildered. The whole aspect of the political and spiritual firmament changed. A new, bright, era dawned upon the history of this land of the Rishis.

Guru Govind Singh was brave, generous, loving, and confiding. Ever watchful of the interests of the community that followed his lead he did not confine his sphere of work to their spiritual regeneration. He actively interested himself in their everyday occupations and joined and led them in their struggle to occupy a position of honour in the land that gave them birth. Men followed his lead believing him to be their Spiritual and Temporal Lord, worthy of receiving their unquestioned homage. He was dearer to them than all their earthly belongings. Health, wealth, wife, children, brothers, sisters, friends, relatives—all were believed to be the Guru's gifts. Men who possessed these blessings never failed to express their gratitude for their bestowal. Those that had no relatives and no property were not less happy; for they all seriously believed they were the Guru's sons and thus embodied in themselves all that was good and honourable. "Guru ang sang rahe!" (May the

Guru bear thee company!) was the benediction, most highly prized, with which one Sikh greeted another Sikh, when parting! The Guru, too, on his part was exactly the embodiment of self-sacrifice and courage. If the disciples considered it a privilege to sacrifice their all at his bidding, there was nothing which he, too, did not risk for them. He washed the feet of his disciples, served them with food and, in other ways, convinced them that he was one whose example they could follow, who was not a deified person whom it was impossible to imitate.

One great defect in our national character has been to deify our heroes. When once deified the heroes ceased to be our ideals. No human being could follow in their wake. They became objects of worship; but between them and the worshippers was placed an impassable barrier. Guru Govind Singh strongly resented the title to divinity set up by many a great man before him. He always took care to see that his people looked upon him only as their spiritual father and that their only object of adoration was the Timeless One. He took pride in acknowledging that his victories were due to his devoted disciples and thus inspired them with confidence in themselves.* No wonder, then, that he should have been able to draw together men of diverse castes under one banner of righteousness. No wonder, then, that the hitherto repellent forces should have converged to effect a mighty revolution and men, forgetting their mutual differences, and inspired with one feeling of

* Judh jite inhí ke prasád.

liberating the country from the yoke of a tyrannic rule, should have shown to the world that, rescued from the yoke of Brahmanism, the Indian races were as capable as any body to defend their hearths and homes and that when properly led, they and their descendants could perform heroic deeds which the world's mighty Generals and great statesmen love to recount and admire. No wonder, that the Guru's followers should have faced the aggressive Islam with the stern command:—"So far and no further*!"

---

* *Agar na hote Gurú Govind Singh sunat hotí sab kí*! Bulleh Shah.

But for Guru Govind Singh all would have been circumcised.